What people are saying about

Spirituality Will Save the World

An important look at the journey of awakening, seen through the lens of the author's own personal journey, a journey that is ongoing.
David A. Teed, LCSW

Spirituality Will Save the World is a highly readable and easy-to-grasp take on the fundamentals of living a spiritual existence, designed to be a welcoming entry point for those interested in consciousness.
Kyle Miller, Kyle Miller Yoga

Spirituality Will Save the World

The Beginner's Guide to Self-Realization

Spirituality Will Save the World

The Beginner's Guide to Self-Realization

Sally Smith

BOOKS

Winchester, UK
Washington, USA

JOHN HUNT PUBLISHING

First published by O-Books, 2021
O-Books is an imprint of John Hunt Publishing Ltd., 3 East St., Alresford,
Hampshire SO24 9EE, UK
office@jhpbooks.com
www.johnhuntpublishing.com
www.o-books.com

For distributor details and how to order please visit the 'Ordering' section on our website.

Text copyright: Sally Smith 2020

ISBN: 978 1 78904 807 0
978 1 78904 808 7 (ebook)
Library of Congress Control Number: 2021931439

A CIP catalogue record for this book is available from the British Library.

Design: Stuart Davies

UK: Printed and bound by CPI Group (UK) Ltd, Croydon, CR0 4YY
Printed in North America by CPI GPS partners

We operate a distinctive and ethical publishing philosophy in all areas of our business, from our global network of authors to production and worldwide distribution.

Contents

To Caitlin, for showing me the portal.

Preface

I feel an inward call from a soul that knows no bounds. It is a determined soul, one that cares deeply for humanity. The communication is sometimes hazy, but this I know for sure: I am here as a vehicle for my soul to perform its mission. This book is my first attempt at that.

Saving the world doesn't start with politics or social upheaval, but rather a shared sense of connection and unity. The root of spirituality lies in understanding. By developing a solid spiritual foundation, the practitioner will naturally effect positive change throughout the social systems in which they operate. Saving the world seems like a complex task, but if I have learned anything from the complexities of the universe, I know that simplification is key. We, as human beings, and more importantly, the upcoming generations, need to first cultivate our spiritual foundation by practicing understanding and acknowledging the whole. From here, our inner work will radiate outward and we will, in fact, save the world.

Acknowledgements

I'd like to thank all those who paved the way. Nevine Michaan and Abbie Galvin who passed along the teachings and techniques to Kyle Miller, Sian Gordon and all the teachers at Love Yoga, my first home in Los Angeles. To Caitlin Malley who helped me unravel my narrative. To Andrew Zamora for being himself. To David Teed and his impeccably timed wisdom. To M.M. who taught me how to use energy and connect with Spirit and to all my guides, teachers, and spiritual forum. You are equally as important as those embodied.

These are the people who guided me through this phase of learning, growth, and evolution, and are therefore the reason that this book was made possible. I thank you all deeply.

Introduction

The term "spirituality" gets a lot of eye-rolls and mixed meanings in today's world. Does it have religious connotations? Do I have to believe in God? Does spirituality mean doing ayahuasca with a shaman named Airbender in Peru? The answer is yes and no—it depends on your perspective. Perspective is a big thing that we're going to address within the pages of this book, so let's define it now and further explore it later. **Perspective: n. A particular attitude toward or way of regarding something; a point of view.**

Each and every one of us has a unique perspective that gauges the way that we view and interact with ourselves, our environment, and others around us. This perspective is often shaped by our upbringing, our experiences, and the people we interact with day in and day out. This leads me to one of my biggest points—if you walk away from this book with nothing else but this sole lingering thought, then I'll consider my entire existence worthwhile. Here it is: you cannot judge anyone else's perspective. It is a product of their own unique experience.

Metaphorical Analysis Alert!

You are a tiny seedling that was picked up by the wind and dropped somewhere on the earth.[1] The wind blew you there and you can't help which way the wind blows! Wherever you were dropped off, well, welcome to your new meadow. Maybe you were dropped off in France and your meadow consists of bread and wine and handsome men named Jean-Jacque LeBeaux. Perhaps you were dropped off in an Indian slum, plagued with homelessness and disease. Maybe you were dropped off in Boonville, Missouri, to a single-parent household; your mother is an alcoholic and your dad left before you were born. Obviously, these hypothetical meadows are going to shape you in one way or another and they most definitely will contribute to the varying outlooks that each meadow might evoke.

The point is that for the sake of this argument—and I will contradict this later—you cannot choose the circumstances in which you were blown into; however, it is those very circumstances that shape your perspective. Therefore, at least *at first*, might we say that you cannot control your perspective? Might we say that you were actually born into your belief system? We cannot help where the wind blows us, but it is that meadow and those other flowers, grasses, and trees that shape us into grown-ass adults that go out into the world to exercise and exert our perspectives in new meadows. *And then*, the cycle continues as these new meadows further mold and shape how we view both ourselves and the world. Coming full circle, this wacky meadow metaphor is simply an anecdote to prove that **we are what we experience.**

If you liked that analysis—good. Because in this book, you're going to come across a dash of philosophical ideas here, a sprinkle of esoteric dialogue there—just certain bits and pieces to keep the conversation ignited without diving deep into MLA or APA cited sources.

So, let's clear up the stigma. Spirituality has nothing to do with which herbs Gwyneth told you to put in your morning smoothie. It has nothing to do with whether or not your mandala was blessed by an Indian sage or how your yoga teacher "became one with the earth" while on mushrooms in Bali. It does not have to involve "the big man upstairs" or require that you be baptized and forgiven of your sins. What these have in common is that they are all some presumed mandate dictated from an external origin that thinks it has control over your spiritual acquisition.

Spirituality has nothing to do with what anyone else is doing and everything to do with the ways in which you access your Higher Self. The notion of your Higher Self is multifaceted. You can view it as anything from attaining your personal ideal all the way to the manifestation of your energetic soul-Self. Your Higher Self is what you attain by setting forth on the path towards Self-realization, a concept that makes up the backbone of this book. Self-realization, just like the term Higher Self, is whatever you need or want it to be. For the sake of this introduction, let's just say that it is any form of inward exploration that allows for personal understanding and betterment. It will vary from person to person and the strategy to attain that Self is based off of the individual's perspective. My version of my ideal self will look different than yours, so our paths in getting there will require different spiritual practices.

These practices are broad in scope and some might not even necessarily seem "spiritual" on their surface. But remember, that designation is up to you. Your next job is to determine what makes up a true spiritual practice. I'm going to give you a very simple question that you can ask yourself but you must approach it with genuine honesty and deep reflection: In whatever "spiritual practice" you engage, is the intention for external validation or inward exploration?

Say that you want to sign up for a yoga teacher training. There are an abundant amount of reasons that you might sign up: to make new friends and build a sense of community; to get the groundwork to become a yoga influencer on Instagram; to create connections for the wellness app that you have in beta; or to simply understand the underlying philosophies of the practice that has given you so much joy. None of these scenarios are any worse than the next, but when it comes *specifically* to spirituality, just understand the differences between external and internal motivations. All sound like valid reasons to do the training, but learning more about a philosophy that brings you joy sounds the most like a truly spiritual practice.

You'll find that people like to use the term spirituality to uplift their own ego—a cover for extrinsic motivations like money or fame. We're not going to do that. That behavior is a major reason that this word and its notion are so stigmatized. You're either a Venice Beach pop-spiritualist, a dirty hippie with dirt-caked toenails, or a Burning Man wannabe who did LSD that one time. This is our problem—because this idea of spirituality has devolved in so many different directions over the past few hundred years, we've found ourselves in a weird time where it somehow permeated into very particular spaces such as the health and wellness scene. Self-realization has always been an inward practice, but now, in the same way that the Church has a history of capitalizing off its believers,[2] some "spiritualists" are doing the same with targeted ads on Instagram and jars of herbal "Chakra Blends" for eighty bucks a pop. Spirituality is for everyone and should be accessible without being stereotyped.

What we're doing here is an inward journey and being able to recognize what underlies an internal motivation is a crucial lesson. On that note, it's also just a good idea to know the true intention behind any action. That way, you know exactly what you're getting out of any particular practice and you can look back to see whether or not that intention was achieved and if that practice actually worked. That way, you don't waste your time in the future. If your intention, however, is to gain a mad Insta-following then go for it! This hypothetical yoga training sounds like the way to do it.

Key Takeaway
Spirituality doesn't ask anything of you. By engaging in a spiritual existence, you learn to ask something of yourself.

The Journey Inward
Inward exploration simply asks that you spend some time focusing on yourself in order to learn, grow, and evolve. Investigate and reflect on your emotions, your reactions, your habits, and your beliefs and consider them in a space that is totally removed from

external influence. A few good overarching questions to ponder might be: What circumstances have shaped me? What patterns exist in my life that beg to be acknowledged and why? Who am I when every external idea, concept, or material thing is stripped away? In what areas can I do better? What can I contribute to the betterment of my community, my city, my country, or the world?

This is called "big picture thinking" in regard to yourself in this time and place.

So, how do we do this? It's a good question because it certainly isn't easy. As you continue on your own spiritual path of Self-realization, you will cultivate tools that help you uncover information and navigate your internal and external environments. For example, therapy: an amazing tool for self-reflection. Other tools: meditation, jogging, yoga, gardening, writing, campaigning, smoking, tweeting, rock climbing, dancing, making a pie, etc., etc., etc.—do you get my point? The tools will be your own and the way you utilize them is subject to your understanding. Anything that you do, if it provides personal insight, can be used as a tool—a spiritual practice. Obviously, in the grand scheme of things, some tools might work better than others, but again, only you can decide what works and what doesn't.

Metaphorical Analysis Alert!

Surfing was one of my primary tools for the entire time that I lived in California. The use and purpose of surfing will definitely differ from surfer to surfer, but for me, surfing is the best when you go out early on a glassy morning just when the sun is rising. It's maybe 5:30am. I am on my 9'0 longboard, an easy-rider, catching waves maybe 2-3 feet tall. Effortless. Certainly a healthier form of escapism and a reminder of just how beautiful the earth is when you look over the horizon and see only ocean. It's a rare feeling of being completely alone while deeply connected. Out there, I get the enveloping sensation of being wrapped up by landscape and I get to feel so small yet powerfully powerless. This is the tool I use to find the clear-headedness and freedom that comes with a vacation only twenty minutes up the PCH. It brings me immense joy which keeps my perspective open and bright, and it constantly reminds me of the greater forces at play.

Okay, but here's the thing: When I go out on a choppier day—when the waves are frighteningly too big for me—surfing becomes a different kind of tool. When I am caught in the impact zone, paddling my hardest to get to refuge, swearing out loud between turtle rolls and rolling whitewash, my emotions swelling like the waves in front of me, I decide that I hate surfing. Once I am through to safety, however, watching the water form crests beneath me, I quickly forget that, moments ago, I was choking back saltwater in between cries of furious swearing. I am able to see how completely unstable and manic I can be when I am knocked off center. In this moment, surfing becomes a lesson in how to minimize my extreme emotional fluctuations or a way to practice resilience. Sometimes I simply learn that yelling and screaming, despite the adrenaline-fueled rush it gives me, doesn't actually get me to safety. I learn how to better apply my energy.

In the end, whatever we decide to engage in and however different it may be from someone else, the lessons are always present when we choose to acknowledge our reactions. When these lessons are learned and applied, then we've found ourselves a spiritual practice. This is how we engage in a spiritual existence. This is how we work our way towards personal betterment— unique in application and dependent upon our perspective—but better nonetheless.

Navigating This Book

I want you to view this book as one of the tools in your toolbelt. Some ideas might resonate with you and bring you joy while others might contradict your belief system and throw you into a furious rage. Take note of your reactions. While you are in between these two covers, I ask that you put your current belief system aside and maintain an open mind. An open mind allows you to soak in information, turn it over in your head, then, either accept it into your understanding or disregard it. It allows you to be conscious while sitting with new information so that whatever you decide to do with these pages is deliberate and a product of *your* own thoughts and nobody else's. You can still reap something out of this book even if you don't subscribe to the overarching themes; so, in the effort of learning, growing, and evolving, give it a shot. Widen your perspective. That's my call to action.

I reference a lot of external sources throughout this book and I want you to know that I'm not just pulling this information out of my ass. It's written over and over again across the texts in various religions from thousands and thousands of years ago. We're talking BCE, baby! The *Tao Te Ching*, *The Bhagavad Gita*, Buddhist scriptures, and more. These aren't your *Live, Laugh, Love* quotes of spiritual wisdom that are pasted all over walls both virtual and stucco. No, these guys go back ages, and although the lines of spirituality and religion will commingle, we will see common threads emerge across *all* perspectives. To me, that proves their truth—that all over the world throughout time, sages, writers, and scholars have received the same messages and come to the same conclusions about the meaning of life and the mysteries of the universe. That is why I trust them. There is a source of divine understanding and a root of all knowledge.

Many writers have so beautifully utilized these teachings in their own work, but for my purposes, I want to provide you with evidence from the earliest and purest sources—the texts and scriptures themselves. That being said, I do throw in a few more modern takes here and there but all are worthwhile and contribute to the overall message. This book, however, is less about me replicating others' words and more about integrating the knowledge from various different backgrounds in one fun and easy read. For this very reason—my nerdy obsession and desire to share this material—I've provided you with a recommended reading list at the back of this book for all your further explorations. These are the writers who taught me everything and I beg you to read their books so that you, too, can soak up all of these incredible scholars' and authors' knowledge firsthand. By doing so, you will *quite literally* blow your own mind.

And finally, this book is a product of personal study. Part of my studies include utilizing spiritual guides and teachers to help me filter and navigate this information. That being said, some of this information has been channeled to some extent. Like any translation, the language of the spiritual and the physical are simply different. I do my best to interpret the meanings in a way that makes the most sense beneath my lens of understanding. Of the information that has been channeled, I include it here because it has helped me illustrate meaning behind the more complex and ambiguous ideas. Plus, whoever is giving me this information, presumably my personal guides and teachers, are incredibly good at breaking down this information and deserve to be acknowledged.

Rev Your Engine

We're about to go on a journey together, so I think it's important that you get to know your travel buddy. I am no expert, but I consider myself an explorer. After I discovered this material, I have since made it my life's mission to continue down the path of learning and discovery. I've had a lot—*a lot*—of help along the way. Spirituality and the establishment of my belief system has given me a profound sense of security and footing in this world. It has helped me expand my perspective and uncover my potential. It has made me aware of the fine orchestration of the universe—the awe and the wonder of it all—and has proved life and existence to be more magical. I only wish the same for you.

The universe is vast and mysterious, and unfortunately, we won't even begin to scratch the surface; but as a beginner myself, I will do my best to make the information easygoing and digestible. It's meant to be fun and exploratory, not overwhelming and dense. Have a notebook nearby to write down your thoughts and insights. If these concepts seem new and overwhelming, slow down, and just have fun with it. Take whatever resonates and then go out on your own to continue your discoveries.

My perception of the world is fluid and changes constantly with every new piece of information that I excavate. This book is a survey of my current understanding.

And while I care deeply for you, I am also on a personal mission here. What I hope to gain from writing this book is my own integration of this knowledge and the words by which to share these lessons. On a more universal level, I want to do whatever I can to raise our collective frequency by asking you to question your perspective. I don't care what you believe, but I do care that we, as a community of human beings, learn that polarization is a product of Earth, and thus, a natural pattern within our existence. Not everyone is going to see things your way. There will always be differences. In working between two extremes, one thing is for sure, which is that extremes are mediated by a common force. I think that that force is understanding. I call it Divine Amnesty. So let's do this. I am stoked. Let's nerd out on things that have forever seemed so serious, but in reality, they don't need to be. Let's bring it down to earth and make it our own. Although forever mysterious, let's shed some light on some universal wisdom and open our minds to the infinite possibilities.

To-Ponder List

It's very important to know what you believe. Having a firm belief system gives you a lens to not only perceive the world, but also a playbook for how to act in it. For me, it gives me a really calming sense of safety. An open-minded belief system is constantly changing the more you learn and explore.

- **Define your belief system.** If that seems too broad, start with writing about your past experience with religion or spirituality. Have you ever questioned those experiences? Why are you reading this book? Do you believe in an omniscient force? God? Energy? Nature? How do you view the world and humanity and what do you hope for the future?

Throughout this book, you will engage in a personal excavation. These questions were mentioned in the previous introduction, but now you have a chance to really reflect on them. Where do you stand now?

- **What circumstances have shaped you?** What patterns exist in your life that beg to be acknowledged and why? Who are you when every external idea, concept, or material thing is stripped away? In what areas can you do better? What can you contribute to the betterment of your community, your city, your country, or the world?

Part One

Chapter 1

Spirituality Versus Religion

There is a movement out there that wants to separate the term spirituality from religion to ensure that they exist in two different categories, and I must say, I see why. Even though much of religion lies within spirituality, let's clarify some history before we move forward.

Before institutionalized religions and before the Church, there were ancient sages (scholars, philosophers, shamans, and holy men) who were deeply connected to Spirit. Through practices such as meditation, they were able to acquire wisdom from advanced energetic sources in nearby realms. Like a psychic receiving a download, these sages were able to connect with higher beings in the joint mission to aid humanity. The lessons they received were universal in nature and spoke of divine knowledge and truth. These messages have been delivered throughout the ages to various people with profound relationships with spirit, and a strong ability to teach and be heard. Some names you might recognize are Buddha, Muhammad, or Jesus, but there have been many notable sages whose teachings have been passed down through the centuries, transcribed, compiled, and later distributed as published texts. In their purest form, these are the lessons delivered by cosmic means.

By virtue of being passed down over thousands of years, however, information has been lost, mistranslated, misinterpreted, or changed altogether to promote a different agenda. Our job is to get as close as we can to the root of knowledge. Without delving into the details of every religion, let's instead start with the oldest texts. The wisdom that you uncover in the Buddha's scriptures, *The Bhagavad Gita* of Hinduism, and Taoism's *Tao Te Ching*, all recount secular ideas—applicable not only to the religious virtuoso but to any earthbound human. These words were not written for a single group or denomination, but for whomever wished to live a more spiritual existence. And the incredibly dope part about all of this is that despite different locations, backgrounds, and religious affiliations, the information received by these sages, *at their very core*, are all eerily similar. Yes, certain tidbits are expanded upon, reimagined, or taken in another direction, but the major themes are the same. This is spirituality. It promotes union rather than divisiveness. It reveals humanity's commonalities. It does not segregate. Unlike religion, it is universal and accessible to all.

The Teachings

As aging and death are rolling in on you, what else should you do but live by the Dhamma [teachings], live righteously, and do wholesome and meritorious deeds.
Buddha

Strive constantly to serve the welfare of the world; by devotion to selfless work, one attains the supreme goal of life.
The Bhagavad Gita

Therefore the wise take care of everyone
And abandon no one.
They take care of all things.
And abandon nothing.
Tao Te Ching, Ch. 27

The Buddha speaks about what is inherent to the human condition. Aging and death are inescapable truths, and no matter our status or condition, we will all succumb to these forces. Buddha's teachings instruct the earthbound human on his way to Self-realization by promoting a moral way of life and doing good by others. *The Bhagavad Gita*, at its core, teaches that by performing selfless service for the whole of humanity, we will attain a worthwhile and fulfilling existence. The *Tao Te Ching*, in a more scaled-back and universal observation of the human condition, teaches us that those who are on the path of Self-realization will be able to realize humanity's innate connection to one another and therefore work to uplift the entire collective as equally as themselves.

The same overarching themes found in the ancient texts can be found within a lot of different faiths, but as years went on, this idea of religion was focused less on the individual and more on the institution.

Each religion has its own dogma—a set of beliefs that you must subscribe to in order to participate. Rather than asking its congregation to open their minds and search for their own truth, they demand that you accept what you are told. In the institution of religion, spirituality is not about an individual's internal search for Self, but rather about external symbols and rituals.[3]

Religion became a tool that people used to gain power or control. Words were rewritten to incite fear among their patrons. Wars were waged and gruesome violence was inflicted. You were told that in order to access God, you must go through the Church. The idea of God became something to seek outside of yourself. Labels were created. You were this or you were that. You were not allowed to question. You were not allowed to believe in the ideas of two separate systems. If you did and you were caught, you were excommunicated or put to death. This is how spirituality morphed into religious divide which morphed into various conflicts that moved the individual and the collective further and further away from the true point: Self-realization.

Notice the polarization happening here. Self-realization, our human goal, is about union—the opposite of which is division. The idea of duality is always going to be present here on earth, but our job is to combat it. Just as there is an energy that promotes union and goodwill, there is also an energy that promotes division and disconnect. Somewhere along the line, the Church got very caught up in that divisive energy. And while many churches don't call for division and disconnect, the idea is still rooted in its history and teachings, so just proceed with caution and intellect.

Don't get me wrong—if you are a religious person, I am not telling you to abandon your beliefs. Religious institutions are powerful when they are used as a tool. If your pastor or rabbi helps you find better ways of interacting with the world and becoming a better person, then utilize it. If going to Church every Sunday gives you structure or a sense of community, use it, baby. You drink that blood of Christ!

All I am saying is be wary of those who try to make you believe that you cannot access God without their assistance—because they're lying to you. These are the people that like to promote their own personal agenda in order to uplift their ego and gain power, money, control, or some personal validation. The religious leaders who know their role and truly want to help and heal are the ones you should seek out. Whether or not you participate in a religious institution, simply by nature of being a human being, you have the power to access God and spirit whenever and wherever you want. You can absolutely live by the words of your religion if those words have proven to guide you towards your own personal evolution, but again, don't be steadfast in your beliefs. Be pliable. Be open. Don't judge. You get to shape your own perspective and it is uniquely yours.

God Damnit!

Let's get past the word God. A lot of us, myself included for a long time, have had a problem with the word God. We associate it with whatever religion that we were brought up in, have since questioned, and is the reason that we are here together reading this book. For many of us, God is seen as this external force who's hard to reach. He's been personified into an old, white, bearded man, sitting atop his golden throne somewhere in the clouds, inflicting both pleasure and pain throughout the world at his own merry will. I don't even know how that happened, but for our purposes, don't be dismayed by the fact that even the ancients use the term "God." Their perception of God is the more pure take on the figurehead and refers to an energy known as the Creator or Origin Source. Whatever energy that birthed the entire universe and stands above all nature, God is that Source. Call it whatever you want though. Call it God. Call it Source. Call it the Universe. Call it She. Call it Marge. It's all the same, so no need to get all caught up in the wording.

So, in resolving the religion versus spirituality question, remember these slight differences. Religion has been tarnished and soiled throughout the years. When we're talking about divine knowledge or truth—the information that wasn't created by man but instead gift-wrapped and delivered to the sages— we're talking about what some refer to as "True Religion."[4] I just like the all-encompassing designation of "Spirituality." Again, don't get caught up in the wording. Just start to practice being fully cognizant of what you believe. Read everything. Question everything. You'll soon cultivate your own belief system that is pliable and able to adapt and change as you uncover more information.

Information is limitless and the longer that you're on this path of Self-realization, the more you will discover. Do not be steadfast in your beliefs, but rather steadfast in the pursuit of knowledge. Take the words of the 1980s NBC public service announcements into consideration when delving into your spiritual pursuits: "The More You Know."[5] Knowledge provides a personal power that not only creates a more lively world around you and takes away the mundanity of a human existence, but it also allows you control over your own perspective—a personal religion if you will. Eventually, the answers that you uncover throughout your pursuit of knowledge will shape the way that you see the world and allow you to better navigate it.

Chapter 2

A Brief History of the Universe

Something mysteriously formed,
Born before heaven and earth.
In the silence and the void,
Standing alone and unchanging,
Ever present and in motion.
Perhaps it is the mother of ten thousand things.
I do not know its name.
Call it Tao.
For lack of a better word, I call it great.

Being great, it flows.
It flows far away.
Having gone far, it returns.

Therefore, "Tao is great;
Heaven is great;
Earth is great;
The human being is also great."
These are the four great powers of the universe,
And the human being is one of them.

The human being follows the earth.
Earth follows heaven.
Heaven follows the Tao.
Tao follows what is natural.
Tao Te Ching, Ch. 25

The universe is like explaining texting to your grandfather—he might pick up on the basics but the vast, vast majority of this strange communication mechanism will remain completely unknown to him for his entire life. I mean, GIFS? There's no way. The universe is so mysterious, so expansive, and so completely impossible for anyone to know or explain. So really, I might be in way over my head.

I'll talk about my personal experience because it's all I have to go by. I often spend my free time at bars or coffee shops, meeting new people, drinking natural wines or macchiatos, while talking about social activism and politics… Okay, wait. No, that's not true. Let me try again.

Before I go to bed at 9pm, I'll often spend my free time under my covers with a flashlight, pen in hand, reading and marking up the pages from ancient, esoteric, and philosophical texts that depict universal ideas from thousands of years ago. From early on in my spiritual endeavors, I knew that I wanted to commit my life to exploring this mysterious entity of the cosmos and share my discoveries with others.

From what I've determined thus far, there are many synchronicities across various religions, philosophies, and ancient myths that place a "why" behind the inner workings of this very complex universe.

Since the dawn of humanity, people have always sought to understand the world around them. In the early days, these people might have been spiritualists, shamans, or sages—ones deeply connected to the heavens or the earth. Later, philosophers, doctors, scientists, and psychologists hopped on the bandwagon in the search for understanding. This quest for truth is innate in all of us. We want answers. We want to understand our surroundings.

When I was young enough for this story to be cute rather than pathetic, my father would tell me that I was born a monkey, picked up at the zoo, and my tail was still kept in the back of the freezer. For years I begged him to just tell me the truth. Obviously, I know I'm not a monkey. I just wanted a definitive answer. I wanted things to be in black and white with no element of uncertainty. Really, I was like eleven or twelve and it was a little pathetic. But hey, us humans are old as dirt and we're still looking for the tail in the freezer. Not only do we want answers — we want clear evidence.

Great segue to one of the most important things that we *must* accept if we want to even begin to scratch the surface of the universe — certain information is simply too high up in frequency, so far from the earthly plane, that we cannot and will not know *everything*. By fully acknowledging this statement, we might be able to relinquish some of that yearning for certainty and find a little more acceptance in the mystery. I've learned to appreciate this uncertainty because it makes the act of discovery so much more exciting.

A Brief Word on Semantics

Before we break it down even further, let me talk about semantics. The human language has come a long way and there is no denying what a useful tool it has become in opening up the doors to better communication. But some aspects of language are incredibly limiting. If I could touch my forehead to yours and you could experience my consciousness exactly the way that I know it to be, there would never be such a thing as a misunderstanding. Language — the catalyst for communication — also creates very many pathways for miscommunication. Especially when talking about ideas that are already quite elusive. Categorizing and labeling creates clear separations that help us recognize the physical world but isn't necessarily helpful when discussing spirit — a topic that actually requires that we break down all of our physical preconceptions. Most metaphysical ideas simply can't be categorized or defined, at least not in this earthly realm.

Unfortunately, we can't touch foreheads to convey a precise meaning, so in order to combat this — clarification is imperative. Because you're reading a book, unfortunately, you won't be able to just pipe up and ask a question, so take everything with a grain of salt. When you're discussing these ideas with others, however, practice clarification. This is something that will also help your overall communication skills. No more misunderstandings with your partner about what she meant when she said, *"I don't want to do this anymore."* She was talking about cutting the onions! You know, when you were cooking that HelloFresh meal together.

Spiritual ideas break down our constructs of time and space, which is something our mind isn't used to grappling—remember, our mind *loves* categories and labels. The language used might not be exact but it will help us paint the picture that we need to see and allow us to better conceptualize complex ideas.

Back to it: The Universal Break-Down

Here we go. At the top, or the furthest away, there is a governing, overarching force that we can refer to as Source energy. AKA God. AKA Creator Source. AKA Marge. So right here—a perfect example of how semantics get confusing. First off, this energy would not consider itself "at the top," as it doesn't occupy space. It also might not consider itself as a "governing" force, because there is no hierarchy in spirit, but you see how these words simply help illustrate meaning. Because words sometimes suck, another tool we can use to better our understanding is in utilizing universal ideas and essences. For example, the essence of a puppy is cute, cuddly, and innocent. Place a puppy in front of five people from five different countries speaking five different languages and they will all come to the same conclusion. We can do this with spirit too.

When something is so overtly complicated, we simplify it by looking at patterns, archetypes, or universal law. In the case of the universe, we can make it as easy as one, two, three. Also known as sacred geometry, this is a type of universal language that is so ancient and so pure that it holds up over time.[6] Each number, one through ten, has an archetype or a representative essence that can help explain some fundamental structure of the universe. Without getting too complicated and eliciting you to close this book and never return, we will only look at numbers one, two, and three.

The gist of the number one is depicted in our *Tao Te Ching* excerpt where, *"something mysteriously formed."* One is Source. One is the creator. One is our origin. It represents the whole and it carries within it the entirety of the Universe. From one—a single point—we're able to draw a circle that expands equally out from its center in every direction. Flashback to middle school math class with your compass and protractor. This center is like our home base where energy moves outward in every direction.

The wheel, also represented by the circle, symbolizes the movement of cycles. The nature of a cycle is its beginning, middle, and end followed by a new beginning. This ultimately directs our awareness to the repetition around us. The circle tells us that the movement of the universe involves an outward and inward cycle of expansion and contraction. The epicenter of this movement is the Creator Source, whose energy ebbs and flows within the dance of the cosmos.

Our internal functioning is a representation of the bigger scale systems. In the same way that the universe moves inward and outward, so do you. Take a look at your own life and recognize the times characterized by extraversion, growth, and expansion; then, look at the times characterized by introversion, calm, and reflection.

Now let's talk about *two*. The main thing you need to know about the number two is that it gives us polarity. *One* tells us that we move away from Source, *two* tells us that we will return. Polarity is involved in any natural cycle. It is the idea of dual extremes: a positive pole and a negative pole. It is good and evil; day and night; two sides to the same coin.

You hold these same polarities within yourself. You go in and you go out. You get fired up and then you cry into your pillow.

You work yourself into the ground and then you pass out from exhaustion. With extremes like these, we naturally lean to one side so our job is to strike a balance. This is where three comes in.

When two things fuse together, they create a third thing: a couple creates a third, a baby; two hands create a sound, a clap; left Twix plus the right Twix creates the Twix bar. *Three* is the "through-ness." It's a transformation. It is the birth of "the ten thousand things." In scientific terms, three is the conductive path that creates an electrical current between two polarized opposites. Three comes in to create a balance between two extremes. The universe, in its natural cycles, is always seeking balance by mediating dual forces.

You might start to mediate the balance in yourself by first recognizing your extremes and which side you stray towards. We have extremes of emotions, extremes of actions, and extremes in the way we think. Imagine it like a fulcrum. When we are perfectly balanced on each side, we're operating from our center—a place of control. We're less likely to completely tip over because we let something, be it an emotion, thought, or action, get out of hand. So *before* the scale falls wildly to one side—say if you're feeling fired up and angry at the world—invite in something that will tip the scale back towards the center. Perhaps you practice accepting the things that you know, pragmatically, you cannot change. Calm yourself down and redirect your anger towards good. If you're burnt out from a job or a relationship, recognize this and stop working so hard. Practice nurturing self-care. If you feel off, you are off. Become aware of any imbalance and always redirect towards center.

Sacred geometry is not your basic math class. It's certainly not black-and-white thinking. But when we begin to wrap our mind around what the numbers mean, we discover how the essence of their meaning contributes to the bigger picture, whether that be the happenings of our lives, our society, or the entire universe.

Numerology transcends language. So in a way, numbers might demonstrate certain ideas that words cannot—goodbye semantics. Use the numbers to navigate any life circumstance or problem. Make what feels overwhelming, easy to grasp. One, two, and three tell us that the Universe began from a single point; the energy of the universe ebbs and flows outward and inward; and everything in between works under the law of polarization where nature will restore balance between any two extremes.

Real World Example

The lead up to 2020, AKA the year that shall not be named, involved the Black Lives Matter movement, the Me-Too movement, the COVID-19 Pandemic, and enough social unrest to turn even the most hopeful of optimists towards despair. America, a single entity, is on a path leading to further and further polarization between its people. If we look at the pattern of the numbers, we know that when dual forces reach their maximum extremes, nature steps in to create balance. I have no idea when this conflict will reach its boiling point—maybe three months, maybe another hundred years. I do know that there is a fight ahead of us—some effort to be exerted. Humanity, after all, is a part of nature. I hope that when the shift happens we find ourselves in a world defined by tolerance and dignity rather than brutality and hatred, or even worse, extinction. The numbers teach us that some event of rebalance lies ahead of us and this knowledge provides us the insight as well as the motivation to pick a side, be active, and work towards our new ideals.

The numbers are a great way to perceive our surroundings, but there are infinite big picture ways of understanding the universe, more of which we will get to later. These natural and universal laws are true for the cosmos, as well as for the human, as well as for anything in between. Every human carries a soul, a small spark of Source energy, and it is that unwavering light in all of us that longs for its return. The human being is a microcosm of the universe, or as the Tao puts it: *"The human being follows the earth. Earth follows heaven. Heaven follows the Tao. Tao follows what is natural,"* and thus the cycle continues. One, two, and three give us the very basics in universal fundamentals, but of course, it's much more complicated. These same ideas are repeated a trillion times over in the various spheres that make up the heavens, the earth, the human, and anywhere that lies within the scheme of the cosmos. The numbers act as a tool to help us simplify.

Whenever we speak in metaphorical language, it can get well, metaphorical—a little weird, a little gray, uncertain. If you hated reading *The Great Gatsby* and debating what the hell the green light meant, then I get it. There are no black and white answers, and that can be frustrating. The best we can do is apply whatever concepts, whatever language, or whatever metaphors make the *most* sense and allow them to guide our personal understanding even if it is slightly different than someone else's.

With this newfound knowledge, take another read through Chapter 25 of the *Tao*. This is one of the oldest descriptions for the Universe. It acknowledges the mystery, the movement, and how the ten thousand things fit into the whole.

How Universal Wisdom is Acquired

Because the human represents the microcosm of the whole, by coming to know ourselves, we begin to unravel the universe— another way to describe Self-realization. Throughout time, humans on the quest for knowledge and truth realized that through meditation—quieting the mind's incessant activity— they came to understand certain universal truths. We connect to spirit through our consciousness by ascending the earthly plane and recognizing the larger design at play.

In the story of Buddha's enlightenment, upon his renunciation—leaving his family and opting for the life of homelessness—he came upon a tree, sat beneath it, and he meditated. He slowly started to come to know the Four Noble Truths which depicted the presence of suffering, the cause of suffering, the end of suffering, and the path towards freedom called the Noble Eightfold Path. This path was unique in that it did not require that one become a wandering and homeless monk in order to attain enlightenment, but rather it outlined what one could do to end their suffering through a much more realistic means.

This was the Buddha's moment of enlightenment,[7] where he achieved the nameship of the Perfectly Enlightened One. From there, he accepted his role as a teacher and went on to deliver these lessons to anyone that wished to walk the spiritual path.

Many great sages have done the same: Moses, Jesus, Muhammad, etc. You've heard their stories. We can all do what Buddha did—maybe not to the same extent just yet—but we can certainly sit in meditation or any moment of stillness, foster our internal ear, and be receptive to any kind of message that comes through. These messages may be simple in nature and others may give you some more profound personal or universal "ah-ha" moment where you thoroughly integrate some basic truth into your web of understanding. Oftentimes, we have to hear certain information many, *many* times before it "clicks," so be patient and keep listening. A still mind has the power to offer us both contemplation as well as comprehension.

Wisdom is further spread by the teachers. A teacher can come in many forms but the ones that I am talking about are the people that have either received wisdom directly from Spirit or have studied with someone who has. Either way, they have exerted mass amounts of effort to achieve their understanding of the cosmos and they selflessly choose to help others on their own path towards truth. I say selflessly because a real teacher has no hidden agenda and they recognize the work of their soul flowing through them.

The misconception about universal truths is that they are

hard to find. But it's not the wisdom that is hard to uncover—it's practically written down for us in some form or another in every religious or philosophical text. It's the stilling of the mind and the integration of what the wisdom means in accordance with *your* circumstances that is the difficult part. We're looking for comprehension and clarity. We all come to know things in our own unique way, on our own timing. The constant exposure, meditation, and contemplation on these truths are all tools you can use to help you weave the threads of insight into the blanket of your perspective. When this is done, you'll find that you are no longer grasping at information, but rather utilizing it almost unconsciously as you navigate every situation.

I just said quite a lot with very little visual aid so here's an example of the integration of acceptance: For me, one aspect of this integration meant letting go of the small things in order to preserve my energy. Take the DMV for example—not once have I ever gotten anything done there in one single trip. It's a flawed government system, 'nuff said. I can't change it and honestly, I don't care enough to even try. But when I leave knowing that I have to come back with some new form differing *only slightly* from the one that I came in with, I know that old Sally would get into her car, yell and scream and ultimately exhaust herself so much that she has to go home and take a nap. New Sally, after learning acceptance, realizes that no matter how much she cries about it, she still has to return with the new form another day.

Here's the upside of this shift in perspective: One, I didn't drive myself into a rage-fueled hissy fit. And two, maybe I use what would've been nappy-time to call an old friend or even just buy a donut. The point is that I didn't unnecessarily waste my energy on something that I couldn't change.

For a while, you scream about it. Then one day you realize that maybe you *should* practice acceptance and then eventually, *years later*, you actually do. That's the integration process.

A Little Bit About Energy

Energy underlies everything around us—solid matter, ethereal matter, metaphysical concepts, mind-stuff, consciousness—it all derives from energy. I don't believe that the energy itself is either purposefully helpful or harmful; but rather, it's the manifestations of certain energies that can appear to be good or bad. But just as you wouldn't be angry at a wasp for being born a wasp, we instead get frustrated by the sting—the manifestation. And because you can't change the nature of a wasp, we instead learn to protect ourselves.

I'm not going to go too far into this subject because science is definitely not my thing, which is actually unfortunate because discoveries in quantum physics are painting a whole new picture of the universe. Science is catching up to ancient wisdom! Imagine that the universe is a giant blanket—each individual thread is woven together to make up the whole. The threads act as their own vibrational fields consisting of energies that move and spin at different frequencies.

Simplified: There are a lot of different layers of reality—some physical, some partially physical, and some completely nonphysical. What we perceive as matter is really just bundles of energy vibrating at different levels. If this energy vibrates very slowly, it's more likely that it will manifest physically. On earth, the energy is dense and heavy and therefore perceivable to the human senses and so considered solid matter. Like the threads of the blanket, these vibrational fields are woven together. They are not totally separate. We might exist in a physical world, but right next to us there could be a "lighter" realm where energy spins at such a fast pace that it is rarely, if ever, identified by our human vision.

It is not the physicist but the Self-realized master who comprehends the true nature of matter.
Autobiography of a Yogi

We can't see the waves from the Wi-Fi or the air that we breathe, but we know that they are there. The human eye can only detect a fraction of the world around us which leaves a lot unseen and unknown. This unperceivable energy, making up the whopping majority of the universe, is part of the unknown. For me, I'm better at wrapping my head around the ancient and esoteric descriptions of it, but this new scientific perspective might be humanity's path towards tapping into our collective potential. It's already happening presently, but as science and spirituality continue to merge as two equal and codependent forces, I believe that the human species will begin to uncover our hidden past and emerge as a more collective union.

Super fascinating, but again, out of my realm of knowledge, so here it is from my perspective. There are two root universal energies that act in polarity to one another and set the conditions within the entire playing field of the universe: the light and the dark, or perhaps better semantics would be the positive and negative. Because energy makes up only the conditions of the playing field, it is neither good nor bad, it has no motive, and it simply acts within the constructs of its own nature. These energies, however, will manifest in all sorts of ways so it's important for us to learn about them, recognize them, and either utilize or combat them. Let's talk about some of the energies that you are likely to come into contact with every day.

Helpful Energies: We like these guys. They include enthusiasm, inspiration, and support. Times when you have felt "in-flow," like you're crushing it at work and it keeps getting better. You're cruising down that wave face with no obstacles in sight. Here, you're tapping into helpful energy. It's great to practice gratitude and acknowledge your accomplishments when these energies come in.

Resistance Energies: They're the worst, but we've all felt them. Doubt, fear, judgement, stagnation. These energies work with the negative side and can be quite insidious. They creep in on you and sometimes manifest so implicitly that it's hard to even notice them at all. They will test your will and offer an excellent opportunity for growth. So rather than getting defeated, try to recognize these feelings as simply a manifestation of energy and know that you have the power to combat them and protect yourself.

Duality Energies: These energies function as a unit. They are the ebb and flow of universal pattern. A few common ones are: helpful and harmful; create and destroy; ease and struggle. One operates on the side of the positive, and the other, for the negative; but they work off of each other hand-in-hand. With these energies, practice nonattachment. If things are going really great, don't kid yourself in believing that everything will stay that way forever. When you're in a period of struggle, take comfort in the fact that the feeling of ease is just around the corner.[8]

Awareness of these energies is key because it gives you tremendous insight into what is actually going on around you. You feel more in control of your surroundings and less blindsided when the unexpected occurs. Everything is energy, even your thoughts, emotions, and intentions. By understanding these implicit forces, you can exercise a certain degree of power over your physical world by utilizing the positive and learning how to combat the negative.

Good Versus Evil

I've been told that I am a doe-eyed optimist, and yes maybe that's true. I want us all to unite and Self-realize, and seeing the constant polarization around me makes me genuinely upset. With my "love-and-peace" perspective, however, I know that part of my work is utilizing the wisdom even in moments of upset, resistance, and struggle. *The Bhagavad Gita* is technically a war story where the protagonist, Arjuna, receives this divine knowledge right before he charges into combat. So yes, this theory must be used in both the good times and the bad.

I recently dove headfirst into a spiritual mindfuck as I was contemplating good versus evil. Let me very briefly illustrate my stream of consciousness: "If Source energy is 'the Tao,' then it's indifferent to both good and bad energies. Instead, it allows nature to play itself out to restore or maintain balance. The next two underlying energies must be good and evil, or rather, positive and negative energies, who are both at odds against one another in order to take prevalence over the universe. It's a constant struggle. Are souls innately good? Do some souls come from good realms while others come from bad realms and both incarnate to exert their positive or negative will on the world? Are we in a constant simulation in the battle of good versus evil and whoever wins creates the new universe? Has my willful optimism been a waste of time and really the fate of human beings lies with whichever side wins?"

Hi. Welcome to my brain. Here's how I ended up conceptualizing this and metaphorically backing myself off the ledge as I began to question my entire belief system: "First things first, Sally, some information is too high up in frequency to understand here on earth, so don't get too down on yourself and start with what you know." This is often how my internal dialogues begin. "Source energy makes up the highest vibration of the universe, and to attain it, one must err on the side of 'good' and utilize the high vibrational, positive energies.

Negative energy is dense and of a very low vibration. Sure, you can allow it to swarm over you and you can even employ your will by its means, but that's not going to get you any closer to Source. Here is our polarity—good and bad or high vibes versus low vibes. At a certain point, a being that errs on the 'bad,' low vibrational side of things will realize that if it wants to grow and change it must step over to the 'good' and positive side. As a being evolves, it attains a higher and higher vibration, and ultimately gets closer and closer to uniting with Source.

Similarly, if one's consciousness chooses not to evolve it will simply reincarnate over and over and over again, stuck beneath the veil of delusion in this hellish realm of earth (I'm getting ahead of myself, see more in the next chapter). But, don't think of Source as the absolute culmination of good. Source energy actually lies outside the spectrum of nature where good and evil exist; however, it does take a high vibrational being to, metaphorically, cross the bridge and obtain Source. Reaching the realm of Source means pure and absolute freedom from the mental mindfucks that make us question our existence and instead we find ourselves in a complete and total absorption in the realm of truth. And the way that I see it, truth most certainly is a high-vibrational attainment."

So if this internal dialogue makes any sense to you, then we can both agree that good *does* always win. At least in the long-term. Self-realization and our personal evolution is the one thing that actually carries over between lives, and if there is one thing I care about above all else, it's our collective path towards Self-realization. What this really means, however, is that we have reason to be good. Sometimes we get stuck in thought warps that tell us that all our efforts in being good and kind and moral— choosing the hard path over the easy—are meritless. We ask ourselves, what's the point? Our efforts don't need to be noticed or acknowledged because beneath the surface, we are evolving and that should be enough.

The presence of duality and polarization is the yin and the yang of an earthly existence. We're constantly and often unknowingly coming into contact with these positive and negative forces. We can accept this truth of duality but that doesn't mean that we need to be compliant about it. We can choose the side that we want to be on. By erring on the side of good, we will evolve. Simple as that.

Chapter 3

Reincarnation and The Eternal Soul

You speak sincerely, but your sorrow has no cause. The wise grieve neither for the living nor for the dead. There has never been a time when you and I and the kings gathered here have not existed, nor will there be a time when we will cease to exist. As the same person inhabits the body through childhood, youth, and old age, so too at the time of death he attains another body. The wise are not deluded by these changes.
The Bhagavad Gita

Reincarnation! Can you believe it? No more worrying about what happens after death, envisioning a black hole of darkness and nothingness, wondering if your actions will deliver you at the Golden Gates of Heaven or the horrific inferno of Hell. We can all stop saying #YOLO to defend our erratic and irresponsible actions! Thank God. Thank Source?

When I was younger, I associated reincarnation with that of three-headed gods and Buddha's protruding gut. It was a totally foreign concept where if one did bad things, they come back as a toad, or whatever. I grew up going to an Episcopalian church, but not once did I hear or learn about reincarnation. The Bible teaches readers that after death comes "Judgement," which to me, sounds incredibly daunting and like it should be something to fear. But the story seems to stop after Judgement Day. Spirituality expands upon this idea of judgement—or for a better word, let's call it reflection—and then goes on to illustrate the return: the repetition of a cycle. And maybe the concept of reincarnation is illustrated differently throughout various sources, but the same notion is present throughout all of ancient wisdom—that existence doesn't end with physical death.

The Taoists believe that nature, whether it's mother nature or human nature, is designed and operates underneath the same fundamental laws that govern the cosmos: polarity, pattern, and repetition. Polarity is duality or oppositional forces. Think "day and night" or "good versus evil." Pattern underlies the idea that we can rely on the same predictable regularities—It is the morning when the sun comes up. If you cut a tree, you can see the rings. If the water is boiling, it's going to be hot. Finally, the nature of any pattern is that it will repeat. It is morning *every time* the sun comes up. You will *always* see rings in the stump of a tree. Boiling water will *never* be cold.

We can look at the cycle of the seasons to demonstrate the point. Remember tenth grade English class? Robert Frost and learning about the seasons in metaphorical language? It's always the same—the patterns of the seasons mimic the patterns in human nature. It's a cycle working and collaborating on two different levels. Poets and artists use this language constantly because it communicates something universal.

Spring brings birth and renewal, the potential for a new beginning. It's spring cleaning and all of a sudden your mom has dumped your entire closet off at the Goodwill. As summer heats up, so do we. With longer days, the fruits on the trees ripen and mature. We're feeling more active and energized, and we stay out late partying and socializing. Fall brings colder weather. The harvests are done and the leaves have fallen. The sky gets darker. We lose our youthful spontaneity and we enjoy the calm. We begin our descent inward for winter. With shorter days indoors, we cozy up by the fire. We move a little slower and hold our loved ones the closest. We find warmth, solace, and eventually death.[9]

Just like the seasons, we find these cycles in ourselves—who wouldn't get depressed when the sun sets at 4pm? There is no denying the cycles of nature: the seasons; the tides; the phases of the moon; our menstrual cycles; the animal food chain; day becomes night; night becomes day; our own mental and emotional fluctuations. Death and decay create the perfect environment for new life. This is obvious in the carbon cycle. So if everything around us is working within a cycle, some orchestrated system of operation, and these cycles repeat and exist on various levels—then why would the human be the exception? Why would we just stop after death?

And I know any skeptic might come at me and rebut that our physical body goes back to the earth, and thus, participates in the cycle of nature. But keep in mind—these laws work on every level. Whatever we witness explicitly—the physical body—the same thing is happening elsewhere, implicitly. As above, so below.

As Above, So Below

As above; so below. As within; so without. As with the universe; so with the soul.
Hermes Trismegistus

So technically this phrase gets associated with hermeticism which gets associated with occultism which makes people's minds automatically jump to witches and Satan. I call bullshit. Hermeticism, at its root, is a tradition of belief based on the teachings of Hermes Trismegistus, one of our crazy-wise and super cool sages that I keep referring to. It's a tradition of esoteric beliefs that border on both religious and philosophical ideations and are based on the elusive *Emerald Tablet* which Hermes found, studied, and later taught its messages and lessons.

The Emerald Tablet is said to be the word of this dude that went by various names: Thoth in Egyptian tradition; Hermes in Greek myth; and Seth, Cain and Abel's younger brother in Christianity. Some viewed him as a man, others as a god, others as an extraterrestrial. In accordance with ancient history, the legend varies from scholar to scholar, but the thing that we like to see is that this mystifying character has appeared all across the history books.

Considered quite mysterious because no one in the modern world has seen it, *The Emerald Tablet* is said to contain the mysteries of the universe. At its core, the tablet teaches that all is part of the whole and communication with the divine is accessible through meditation. Furthermore, one of Hermes' primary teachings based off of *The Emerald Tablet* was that this essence of "the One" describing the entirety of the universe also exists and is mirrored in the individual. This individual soul will inherently seek to evolve and transcend throughout its reincarnations in order to attain a perfect state. In the teachings of Hermes, *"man is only a temporary carrier of something with a greater purpose."*[10] This is all beginning to sound quite familiar.[11]

This might be a topic that is hard to grasp. For many of us, it goes completely against what we were brought up to believe. If you want to outright reject it, that's okay. Because whether or not you believe in reincarnation, we can all begin our paths towards self-betterment right here in this present life.

So what exactly reincarnates? If the universe expands equally outward from the singular point of Source, then it is that Source energy that is expanding. This is what is referred to as your inner spirit, or soul. It is your Higher Self, that thing with the "greater purpose." I like to imagine that my internal soul, dwelling within my body, is connected to a tiny etheric thread stemming from my occiput all the way to the universal soul of Source.

The soul's mission is to return back home, and in doing so, it follows the universal flow of expanding and contracting. The yogis call it "to yoke" or unite. We do this by acquiring truth or knowledge so that we can evolve. This understanding comes in the form of lessons to be learned, and duties and actions to perform. So, if we're going to explore this idea of reincarnation further, we might ask ourselves: what's the point?

Metaphorical Analysis Alert!

Like a child undergoing her primary education, she starts in elementary school, graduates to middle school, and then goes off to high school. Imagine that each grade is a single life on earth. Each grade presents its own lessons like how to read, how to tell what qualities make a good friend, how to pick yourself back up when someone is mean to you. As you progress, the lessons get more difficult and complex. Each grade presents a different environment to foster new lessons or expand upon old ones. The child will succeed in some areas and probably fall behind in others. Maybe they repeat a grade or skip a grade or simply work a little bit harder on certain lessons the following year. In this particular school, everyone moves at their own pace and no one is pressured by time. Rather than the thirteen ascending levels of Kindergarten through Twelfth, there are thousands of grades that one soul traverses. It's like one of those new-age Montessori schools.[12]

Most of us here on Earth are still in elementary school. Earth is a massive playground for trial and error. We play house, cops and robbers — we even play war.

And you know how I mentioned that some information is just too high in frequency to understand it here on earth? Unfortunately, some of that mystery lies within this concept. We can't be exactly sure of the master plan. We know that every incarnating soul is an extension of Source energy and it seems like we're supposed to experience the world through as many different perspectives as we can in order to evolve. The Buddha tells us that our goal on earth is to eventually free ourselves from the cycle of reincarnation. We return to earth again and again to learn the lessons of being embodied — to live in a far less than perfect world surrounded by almost constant temptations and distractions.

Earth is Hell

From the bottom-up, earth is the densest physical plane. Because it is a physical realm, the energy spins much slower and is therefore of a lower frequency. It's a realm that is particularly attractive to those low vibrational energies. The negative force is strong, y'all! Because of the overwhelming influence of the negative, I might go as far as equating earth to that scary notion of Hell. Here's why:

In Kirpal Singh's introduction to *The Jap Ji*, he describes "the three grand divisions of Creation," also referred to as "the grand hierarchy of creation." The human is divided into three parts: the actual physical body; our consciousness, the part of the mind that includes the collective or universal mind (think Carl Jung and the collective unconscious); and finally, the soul or extension of source. If you've ever heard the saying, "body, mind and spirit," it's the same idea and you might realize that they have very similar associations with these realms.

Patterns or classifications found on one plane can surely be found elsewhere. These three bodies make up the human but they also define the realms. Body, mind and spirit is a classic trinity. Another trinity is the gross, astral and causal realms similar to the concept of hell, limbo and heaven. The gross realm makes up the physical world—souls in skinsuits here on planet earth. Although there are other physical realms too, for our purposes, let's just stick with earth. The astral plane is reachable through our subtle body. You may have heard of astral travel which is where one's second body detaches from their physical body and can explore parts of the world or parts of the astral realm with an ethereal body. This alone is proof that consciousness doesn't end with the limitations of the body. Finally, there is the causal realm which is the realm of the spirit.

Paramahansa Yogananda recounts in his book, *Autobiography of a Yogi*, a conversation with Sri Yukteswar concerning the bodies:

You have read in the scriptures... that God encased the human soul successively in three bodies—the idea, or causal, body; the subtle astral body, seat of man's mental and emotional natures; and the gross physical body. On earth, a man is equipped with his physical senses. An astral being works with his consciousness and feelings and a body made of lifetrons. A causal-bodied being remains blissful in the realm of ideas.[13]

And from a psychological perspective:

Visualize the mind as having three concentric circles, each smaller than the last and within each other, separated only by layers of connected mind-consciousness. The first outer layer is represented by the conscious mind which is our critical, analytic reasoning source. The second layer is the subconscious, where we initially go in hypnosis to tap into the storage area for all the memories that ever happened to us in this life and former lives. The third, the innermost core, is what we are calling the superconscious mind. This level exposes the highest center of the Self where we are an expression of a higher power.
Michael Newton

The last excerpt is from the book, *Journey of Souls*, by Michael Newton—personal guru and mega gamechanger. More on him in the next chapter.

Okay, so fair warning, this concept of the three bodies, realms, layers of the mind goes way deep.[14] It's my understanding that the realms are then further divided by varying degrees depending on which theoretical lens you look through, but the truth lies within the correlation. All signify a degree of body, mind and spirit that accompanies their division. As above, so below. What we can discern is that Earth, on the level of the macrocosm, is the densest physical realm. It's hell. The astral realm carries characteristics of both the gross and causal realms, similar to limbo. There is some degree of physicality, yet we operate through consciousness. The causal might represent heaven as earth's dual opposite.

Right, so let me come back to it: why are we in hell? Look around, the earth is corrupted with wars, natural disasters, and evil leaders. It's *hard* being a human. I think hell is a notion that got corrupted with the Church to instigate fear and demand firm bonds from their patrons, but Hell is derived from the same idea as the realms. Don't fear hell, because you're already in it.

This doesn't mean that Earth is a bad place, it simply has the conditions for evil to manifest and that makes it a really great training ground for souls. All the evil that we see in the world extends directly from that negative energy. Negative energy is dense in vibration so it's no wonder that it likes to hang out here on earth.

If our role is to evolve and ascend, then you can bet that this negative energy is going to create distractions everywhere we look. Media, Instagram, parties, gossip—it's hard to look away! The negative energies present on earth want to keep us here in the cycle of reincarnation by continually creating distractions that keep us from our mission. But don't get pissed at the energy itself, it's only doing what it does. When you're thriving, this energy sees a void of its presence and creeps in to try to fill it. The nature of energy is that it wants to manifest—both good and evil want to exude their presence all over the world so there's a constant struggle at hand.

If we want to fight for the side of the good, then we must learn how to study and understand the manifestations of this negative energy so that we can learn how to combat it. Many of our lessons here on earth are unique to this concept where we must mitigate the distractions caused by the negative in order to reap knowledge and ascend.

So we might not ever get to learn the exact reasoning behind the purpose of our life on earth and reincarnation. And trust me, I have gone on thousands of thought spirals questioning it all. But from the evidence we do have, we can make some inferences. We know that the movement of the universe is expanding and contracting, so we know on some level that our purpose is to return. We know that Source is the energy that makes up "the tao" or "the way"—that it is totally indifferent to extremes and detached from outcomes. Beneath this Creator/Source energy, positive and negative energies underlie every physical, mental, and spiritual manifestation. The spark of Source energy, our souls within us, yearns for union within the realm of pure knowledge and truth.

What I've explained here is simply where I am currently in my understanding, and honestly, it might change tomorrow. I have no idea why we live out these lives again and again under such varying and specific situations. I do, however, recognize that each life, each body, and each circumstance allows us a different playground and a new perception of humanity and the world around us. Each life—the chance to walk in a different pair of shoes—in a way allows our soul to truly live out every physical, mental and spiritual circumstance. These experiences underlie the foundation that promotes understanding.

A Short Note on Trinities, Nature's Threesome

Trinities are dope. They're everywhere. The third gives birth to everything and it makes up time and space (literally—past, present, future and length, width, height—they all come in threes). True trinities replicate the universal law of three where at first there is a singular force; a second force creates duality; and the connection between these two forces creates a portal, where something new is gained between two extremes ultimately creating some semblance of balance. The body is grossly physical and dense. Spirit is light and luminous. The two together create extremes that are connected by consciousness—

accessible through the physicality of the mind but a portal to the spirit. In the same way, the astral realm connects the physical to the causal because it proves that consciousness does not require a physical body. Through the portal, we glimpse into our nonphysical existence. Trinities go back to sacred geometry. They help us understand certain patterns of energy in the world around us. The trinity is the essence of balance.

Carl Jung gets it.

But every tension of opposites culminates in a release, out of which comes the "third." In the third, the tension is resolved and the lost unity is restored.
Carl G. Jung

To-Ponder List

Take a moment to acknowledge how energy manifests for you. Because energy is quite subtle, it finds ways of interacting with you through various means, be it people, thoughts, emotions, environments, words or objects.

- **What energy is attracted to you?** Do you often find that you cycle through the same sorts of thoughts? What about people who are attracted to you? Self-deprecating? Egotistical? Optimistic? If any pattern emerges, this energy is attracted to you and it continually finds its way to you.
- Now that you have some awareness of the energy that is attracted to you, **decide what you want to do with it.** Thought drives energy. Simply ask for it to leave you alone, or better yet, visualize yourself in a protective sphere that this energy cannot penetrate. If there is any particular energy that you find limiting, it's important to set up protection practices for yourself.
- **Intuition:** n. A thing that one knows or considers likely from instinctive feeling rather than conscious reasoning.
- **Have you ever had intuitive thoughts or ideas that you later realized benefited you in some small or major way?** Do you have a strong ear for intuition?
- **Where do you believe that those thoughts came from?** Your soul? Your psyche?

Part Two

Chapter 4

Your Soul and Your Path

Let's talk about you—your soul, that is. Can you feel it flickering within you? That sucker can feel pretty deep, but you do have access to it, and the longer that you're on this path of knowledge, the better you get to know your soul.

Really quickly, let's clarify some ideas about Self-realization, or for better understanding, you may want to call it Soul-realization. Some call it God-realization, but it's all the same. We throw a fat capital "S" on it because it represents not yourself, but your Self—the Source energy that extends through you. It's that superconscious level that almost lies undetected within you, except for the fact that to some degree, intrinsically, you acknowledge its existence in the same way that on some level you recognize that there is a higher power in the universe, whether it be the gods or the oceans.

All souls wish to become Self-realized, even if the human doesn't recognize it. To set out on the path of Self-realization means to commit yourself to personal discovery. It requires going inward and recognizing your habits and thought patterns, your strengths and your weaknesses, your beliefs and your orientation. Then, you actively and consciously deliberate on them in order to become a version of your ideal Self. This Self is one that thinks and acts unperturbed by outside influence and maintains a steadfast moral code by which to live. This is the path of learning that we can choose here on earth and when achieved, even to a micro-degree, will promote personal and soul growth.

Every life that the soul is born into creates a first nature— how the human views the world and how they choose to act in it. Parents, for example, chosen by the soul, exhibit a large amount of influence on that child's initial perspective or first nature. As we recall from the meadow metaphor, the human has no power over the life and circumstance that they were born into as well as the views and behaviors that they adapt. The human's soul, however, knows exactly why they picked a certain situation, be it location, body type, or family members. These initial circumstances create our primary lessons.

A little about me: Born into a family of four, I was the baby, and that makes five. I grew up in the capital of the confederacy where politics aligned with tradition. I was a very independent child, often exploring the neighborhood on my own from the early age of five or six. I never witnessed intimacy between my parents and they later got a divorce. A typical punishment was to be sent outside. I remember googling legal emancipation, holing up in my room and taking shots of Smirnoff flavored vodka. My eleventh-grade essay argued how a bad childhood only guarantees a better adulthood. I thought and acted in ways that were direct reactions to my environment without understanding the underlying effects of my circumstance.

When I started therapy, I uncovered a different story: I never had much emotional support and I was very lonely. My parents shouldn't have gotten married, proven by the divorce, and their split tore away what was left of any lingering feelings of love and openness, and in its place, left oftentimes overwhelming manifestations of greed, sadness, and tension. The house concealed secrets of abuse unacknowledged by passivity. Nothing that I was taught from my environment fit into the stereotypic mold of what it meant to be a family making my entire adolescence an ambivalent affair. With an added awareness of the underlying structure, I realized I was left with a first nature narrative that I was betrayed and abandoned, that I was my own sole caretaker and that I wasn't to trust anyone to help me. My existence alone was a burden to others so I learned to tread carefully and not piss anyone off. These were the beliefs that I formed in reaction to the situations around me and how I learned to cope.

Most of our deepest patterns stem from the reactions from our childhoods. So, the work begins with awareness. Through awareness, I decide that I no longer want to operate under the misinterpretations of my first nature, so I actively work to change my thinking. This is called a second nature—the difference being that I *choose* how I want to respond rather than reacting. This choice reflects the creation of a new personal narrative. I may fear abandonment, but I know I am worth loving. I am fiercely independent but it's okay to ask for help. I'm simply not a burden. It's a cycle of **reaction, awareness, and re-creation,** where you get to decide what to make of yourself.

This is how I unraveled my personal history, but you have one too. I know that I generalize it in a way that sounds easy enough, but the day-to-day of working through these processes is incredibly challenging, sometimes depressing, and oftentimes very overwhelming. Don't forget that when you're deep in the work. This all relates to the soul because the soul chooses it—I chose this life and the personal narratives that are the hardest to rewrite are surely all a part of my primary lessons. These are the areas in which I need to grow, generated out of past experience, that will allow me to become my ideal Self.

When you choose to embark on the quest of Self-realization, you begin to cultivate your third nature—the constant continuation of bringing forth information that was once unconscious and consciously recreating it. So it's like integrating that cycle of reaction, awareness, and re-creation into your everyday life. I can make the assumption that my soul chose this existence for *whatever* particular reason. I can trust the mystery of that reasoning because I trust the universe. Nothing is random. There is no such thing as a coincidence. My soul knows what it is doing and as long as I maintain awareness and constantly recreate myself towards a better ideal, I know that I am putting in the work.[15]

I think back to that eleventh-grade essay where I believed that hard childhoods guarantee easier adulthoods—unfortunately, that's not the case. In my experience, life only gets easier if you put in the effort. It's not a profound paradox—anything great has never come easy. The path of Self-realization is intended to induce a personal understanding which leads you towards ease within. Yes, it is very hard work, but it is also very worthwhile.

The Work

I keep using this term, "the work," so I want to clarify. The specific outline of the work is very personal to ourselves and our souls' vocation, but in a broad sense, the work is the actual effort that we put into our self-betterment. It's *how* we strive to be more. For many of us, our work can very simply be discovering our own concept of morality and ethics and implementing it daily. Whether we view the soul in this process or not, most likely that inner mission of the Higher Self is going to manifest in our most innate desires. That's just how the soul works. Sometimes it's quite explicit, screaming at us through our inner ears; other times it works much more quietly, whispering sweet nothings to us while we dream.

We react to our environment. We observe and become aware of our reactions. We recreate ourselves by deciding how we want to respond to our stimuli. The act of becoming aware and recreation is how we do our work. If our work is digging a hole, it's easier with a shovel. Similarly, if our work has something to do with diminishing our ego, we might take up boxing in order to get a healthy ass-kicking and practice some dang humility. There are ample tools out there for us to discover and develop that will help us engage in our work. The work is challenging, but we learn to work smarter, not harder, and by doing so, we make it a little easier on ourselves.

The soul is the piece of us that lives on after death. It manifests in a body every now and then but lives in its permanent home somewhere in the cosmos. While many texts speak of reincarnation, rarely do we find accounts of what happens in the in-between. Enter Michael Newton, PhD, psychologist, hypnotherapist, and teacher. Now deceased, but wow did he do some excellent work in past life regression and uncovering what truly happens after death. His legend lives on at the Michael Newton Institute in California. I know he's dead, but I still have a major crush on him.

A skeptic himself, Newton inadvertently discovered a portal to the in-between, or spirit world, during one of his past life regression sessions with a client. After obtaining an initial account, he slowly developed his research and ultimately published *Journey of Souls*, which is a collection of case studies recounting the various dynamics within the world of spirit. This is the first book I read that truly opened the doors to everything else and a highly recommended read.

In brief, the spirit world is our true home. We have friends, soulmates, guides, and masters, all of whom hold our highest interests at heart—our evolution. In a new school metaphor, think of the soul world as a classroom and life on earth as a field trip. We're always working on our lessons both in and out of the classroom. The field trip, however, gives us an immersive experience that really helps us to iron out these lessons in a dynamic and nuanced way. In our soul world, we have an omniscient perspective and we do not operate under the constructs of time or space. From this vantage point, we are able to reflect on all of our lives at once, enabling us to see how our personal growth has played out all across the board. Embodied and on earth, we're lucky if we can even consciously gauge a handful of our lessons. In the soul world, we get to look over the entire syllabus.

Time spent in the soul world is mostly spent in reflection

and preparation. We reflect upon the life just lived, the lessons achieved, and the gaps where we could've done better. We can revisit certain chapters and practice alternative scenarios. It's like your lacrosse coach playing back film after a game to see how certain plays were a success and where the others went wrong.[16] In addition to reflection, we also prepare for the next field trip. We study, we do research, and we ultimately begin to make decisions for our next life that will be conducive to our learning. When we're ready, our soul drops down into a new vessel.

None of this is done alone. Unlike the physical realm, driven by the ego, in the soul-world, everyone wants what is best for you. There is no competition and no hierarchy, only love and understanding. We have guides who act as our teachers, instructing our learning and maintaining a close presence with us throughout our lives on earth. We also have what Newton refers to as our primary soul-group. These are the souls that make up our true family and who will typically reincarnate as significant figures during an earthly life in order to help us achieve the lesson. This can be a little scary because you might worry that the people you love here on earth aren't as close in the spirit realm. I don't think it's worth getting hung up on though—when you're in the soul state, none of that matters. Furthermore, there is the secondary soul-group which is simply an extension of the network of souls with whom we often reincarnate. We all have karma—past action, both positive and negative—between each other, so we live lives on earth together in order to work out our karmic debts.

Again, all of this is described in much greater detail in Newton's books as well as with various other authors on past life regression. The soul world is dynamic and complex. We cannot expect to understand every aspect, but through these regressions, we have gotten a lot of information on certain intricacies that may or may not bring you a sense of ease.

When I first read *Journey of Souls*, it clicked automatically. I was so stoked to (re)remember this truth about the universe and it brought me a lot of comfort. Naturally, I thought that everyone needed to know so I pushed the book on a few people and I learned the hard way that these ideas cannot be forced. If someone is meant to make these discoveries in their life, then they will in a much more organic way. That doesn't mean that you can't talk about it or recommend certain sources to friends, it just means don't force your boyfriend to read a book as "the only way to understand you," and then show him how you can move a pendulum with your mind. It can be very scary if you're not ready for it, and all-in-all, just not a good idea.

For me, I take comfort in knowing that beneath our differences, we're all souls who purposefully chose this life for whatever particular reason, and that reason is fundamentally good. Every person is placed in our lives for the realization of some lesson, and oftentimes, the bigger the character, the bigger the lesson. I have quite a few really difficult personalities in my life, but they've presented me with some of my biggest lessons. These are my teachers, so I *try* to approach their soul from a place of gratitude even if sometimes I despise their human incarnation. Sometimes when we meet a person for the first time, we recognize them. This is no coincidence—something deeply rooted inside of us remembers.

I love believing in this greater dynamic. It is purposeful and it promotes a sense of understanding for everyone here on earth. This is the essence of my true Self and I feel more connected when I am able to tap into the eyes of my soul—seeing the world with the knowledge of our embedded connectivity.

Even if you don't want to believe it, you have to admit it sounds pretty dreamy. And if you *absolutely* can't believe it—if it's just not clicking—then that's absolutely fine. That doesn't mean you can't still aim to be your ideal version of yourself. Your work will simply be set within the parameters of this life. All efforts reap reward; that's a universal truth. Aim to die better than you were born.

For those of us going along with it, I am sure you're asking yourself, "Why do I have no recollection of any of this?" Why on earth do we experience this amnesia? Why can't we remember our real home, our past lives, our best friends? It certainly seems that this whole notion of lesson-learning would be easier if we didn't have to start from the beginning every single time.

Wisdom and connection with Source or our Higher Self is an inward journey and it takes massive amounts of effort. If we're born knowing, the work isn't really there is it? It's a choose-your-own-adventure story—it's no fun if you know every outcome. This "not-knowing" allows us to first get a little screwed up so that we can consciously recreate ourselves. A critical lesson for all of us in every life is finding the path to Self-realization. This effort might look different from person to person, and it's really not our job to determine who is doing the work and who is not. There is no way to know why a soul chose a certain life. Remember again that inward exploration has everything to do with *you*.

True education is not pumped and crammed in from outward sources, but aids in bringing to the surface the infinite hoard of wisdom from within.
Paramahansa Yogananda

The goal is to Self-realize. Looking inward is the first step. And the more you do it the easier it gets, not only within this life but across multiple lives too. As you begin to journey inward and access the deep well of the universe, the amnesia might begin to fade and that proves you're on the path. You might begin to see past lives or hear the voices of your guides in your head. You might become more conscious of the synchronicities of the universe literally screaming at you to acknowledge something right before your eyes. And if it's not that explicit, we all have intuition. Whenever you've had an instinct that turns out to be correct, that's your soul communicating with you. Start to train yourself to identify that voice. First thought is intuition, second thought is doubt. Don't let doubt creep in. Trust instinct over judgement.

We're all just kids on a playground! The game of life. And just like a game in kindergarten, the stakes aren't too high. We do the best that we can, and at the time of physical death, our soul leaves our body and gets to go home. How fun! You're greeted by guides and friends, all of which are just so happy to see you. There is no fear. No one is going to yell at you saying, "You really screwed this one up," but instead, like your sweet Kindergarten teacher, Ms. Pebbles, your guides will sweetly ask you, "How can you do better next time?" and then they might give you a push-pop.

For real though—as humans on this path, we are constantly battling between two major perspectives. One is the earthly perspective where we feel like we're not good enough, the world is scary, and time is limited. When issues come up, they sometimes feel too big to conquer and we fall into negative energies of hopelessness and despair. We get too attached. The soul-perspective is easy-breezy, baby. Life is a classroom and nothing needs to be taken so seriously. You are deeply loved and everyone wants the best for you. You took on a great challenge by coming to earth, but you did it because you're brave and maybe you enjoy the ocean breeze on your face or the feeling of fresh sheets. It's not all that bad, is it?

Chapter 5

Tools

I think this makes a good transition to finally start talking about the tools. I don't know about you, but I am feeling amped up—a little overly eager. That's typical for me. My eagerness oftentimes gets me into unnecessary situations, so personally, I need some tools to fight impulsivity and hyper-excitement. We can uncover them together here in this chapter.

We all need a little help, and if we're smart and capable, we know how to ask for it. And if we don't know how to ask for it— great! We've got tools for that. To begin, there are really three types of tools that I like to consider: tools that help you cultivate awareness, tools that give you clarity of mind, and tools that help you learn and explore. In this chapter, we're only going to talk about the first two and then Chapter 7 will cover the rest.

Tools are broad in application, and again, any particular tool and its use will be very personal to you. It can be anything from a favorite hobby to a particular type of person to a chunk of clear quartz. Remember the surfing example from the introduction? Surfing gives me both applications: awareness of my unconscious reactions *and* ease of mind.

For the ones that help you cultivate awareness, if you recall from the last chapter, awareness is what happens when you become conscious of your reactions, otherwise known as your first nature. Therapy is a perfect and straightforward example. You go to therapy to work on yourself, perhaps to understand why you think or behave the way that you do. Throughout the process, your underlying narrative unfolds. You might have one of those ever-elusive "breakthrough moments," or more realistically in my experience, I slowly and torturously watch myself unravel until one day on a walk with my dog, I'm smacked in the face with the hand of insight. "Oh, that's why I put up my walls!" Therapy was the tool I used to understand my emotional abandonment, my protective survival mechanisms, and just about everything else that defines my thinking.

Less obvious examples might include dieting, acting, or reading. The way you do one thing is the way you do everything. If you're rigid with your practices, you might be rigid in your life. If your diet involves eating only between the hours of 12pm and 8pm and under no circumstance will you allow some flexibility, not even for your dear grandmother's 99th birthday brunch, it might be worthwhile to notice where else in your life you hold this rigidity. Notice if your belief system, too, is immovable. Perhaps begin to consciously create pliability in your life. In this case, dieting became a tool to become aware of rigidity.

Maybe you find yourself surrounded by stuff: empty Bic pens, countless glass jars, childhood macaroni frames, every baby tooth you ever lost, and you realize, "Yeah, so I'm a hoarder." In this case, hoarding is your tool and awareness teaches you the underlying reasoning behind the hoarding. Maybe you begin to create a better sense of detachment or you learn to lessen your grip on control. I don't know what hoarding specifically means for you. No two hoarders are the same, but the point is that you have the ability to dive a little deeper behind your actions to see the underlying *reaction*.

Let's do one more—that one friend. You know the one. The person you go to every time you want to feel better about yourself. Maybe it's a casual sex-friend and the sex is fun and lighthearted, and because he's just so far from your type, it never fails to produce the element of thrill. Maybe it's just a friend who dotes on you. You're not even that close but they're weirdly obsessed with you and always eager to hang out. It makes you feel good, so what? But now we look at the underlying reaction. What triggered you to reach out to that friend? Maybe you feel undervalued at work or you got stuck in a rough cycle of self-limiting thoughts or you're just bored. Again, I don't know, but you do. The pattern of going to that friend has the potential to ignite some awareness about your unconscious thoughts, beliefs, or behaviors. You might not notice it every time. But with repetition, awareness will come.

Begin to notice how you approach any person, activity, object, or habit, and observe how they reflect back at you. If someone on your team at work constantly irritates you, ask yourself why. Is it something they do? Something you hate? Can you let it go? Or screw you, Karen from HR, you suck. All of these things have the potential to help you acknowledge your first nature when you're able to infuse them with awareness. Once awareness is attained, you can re-create. Maybe stop blazing that loser from college—he still wears his fraternity letters. It's not thrilling, it's arrested development.

I understand that everything I just said sounds very equivocal and way too hypothetical. Unfortunately, because these tools are going to be so personal to you, there really is no way to state it in black and white terms. So let's just summarize:

- The way you perceive anything has the potential to teach you something about your first nature—your unconscious reactions to the world around you.
- Repetition and continually coming back to the same object, person, or behavior will allow you to develop an awareness of that first nature.
- Once you attain awareness, you decide what to do with it. Do you want to change this thought pattern, belief, or behavior? Or keep it—not all unconscious behaviors are bad.

Really simply, it's about noticing the things you do and deciding whether or not you want to change them. You might use some of these tools every day and others very sparingly, but the most

difficult part of the whole process is allowing for awareness—
that hit of insight—to come your way.

Awareness is most easily accessed when the mind feels free
and clear. So, the *most* important tools to have on your toolbelt
are the ones that help you create ease in the mind. Everyone's
methods will be different and it might take some time to discover
which will work best, but I am willing to bet that you can list
off at least one or two tools right now that never fail to bring
you ease. As you continue to interact with people, participate
in activities, own objects, or carry on with your habits, observe
how they reflect back at you, and notice which ones bring you
joy. It's literally the strategy of Marie-Kondo-ing your life.

My top five: escaping into nature, meditation, 60s music
(Grateful Dead, the Mamas and the Papas, the Zombies, John
Denver—dare I go on)?!, eating mushrooms (for medicinal and
spiritual purposes, not always just to party, but yes, sometimes
just to party), my closest friends. All of these bring me mass
amounts of happiness because they give me what I hold closest
in the world. Nature, meditation, and mushrooms remind me
of the broader perspectives. They teach me about the universe
and I am their eternal student. Friends and music are my "quick
hit," if you will. They're easy to access; they provide a burst of
serotonin; they never fail to lift my spirits and the joy that they
give me takes no effort to attain.

Ask yourself what is *the most* important to you. For me,
it's spirituality and universal exploration. When I lose my
perspective, I know exactly what I need to get back on top. If
connection with the land is your top priority, then maybe you go
camping once a month and plant a garden in your backyard. The
mind creates ease out of joy so it is imperative that you know
off the top of your head what makes you joyful. These are your
primary tools and you'll keep them on standby for whenever
you need them. And don't forget your "quick hits." I can't eat
mushrooms every day, but I can listen to John Denver's *Rocky*

Mountain High and feel that the world is going to be okay.

On that note, and worth mentioning—for a while I thought booze and bud were excellent tools to give me what I wanted. And yes, they gave me a pleasant distraction and a super heady escape but maybe not the best tools to associate with joy and ease of mind. But hey, I also take mushrooms for spiritual progression, which some purists in the spiritual world might see as cheating. All I am saying is to make sure that whatever tools you choose *in this context* are used with an intention to achieve your true priorities. Later when you're all doped up and feeling good from your quick hits, you can get yourself a cocktail.

Meditation

In basically all of ancient wisdom, it is said that meditation is the surefire way to Self-realize:

Monks, whatever grounds there are for making merit productive of a future birth, all these do not equal a sixteenth part of the liberation of mind by loving-kindness [Buddha's way of saying meditation].
Buddha

Even one who inquires after the practice of meditation rises above those who simply perform rituals.
The Bhagavad Gita

As for all the tools, meditation is mentioned again and again as the number one thing you can do to achieve Self-realization. It doesn't matter your intention—if you set up and maintain a consistent meditation practice, you will absolutely receive major benefits and massive insights along your path of personal and spiritual growth.

I moved to Los Angeles when I was nineteen and it was there that I became immersed in yoga. I'd consider yoga my initial entryway into this world because, and I didn't realize this at the time, I was actually learning fundamental concepts about sacred geometry, Taoism, and Eastern philosophy. Because I was infatuated with this world and lived to please my teachers, I quickly developed a meditation practice, but it never truly stuck. There was no intention behind it. Once I learned about the soul world, however, I wanted to experience it firsthand and that became my first intention.

Meditation is hard in the beginning, but it gets vastly easier, and then increasingly difficult. In setting up your practice, the hardest part is the consistency; the easy part is when your effort pays off, insights might start downloading, and then all of a sudden in the middle of the day, you crave those moments of stillness. That high is what brings you back time and time again. You might get hooked on it. My meditation practice now has changed and evolved tremendously from where it started only a few years ago. And yes, I, too, am hooked. I want to go further and deeper every single time and rarely do I get what I want. With consistency and curiosity, however, every now and then, I'll get pleasantly surprised.

Back to our trinity of body, mind and spirit—remember, where the physical and spiritual are connected by a common force? In meditation, the mind is our connection. While all mammals have a brain, the human mind is somehow something unique and different. Within it holds the subconscious and the superconscious, our repressed memories from this life and past lives, access to other realms and interdimensional beings, the collective unconscious and so much more. It is quite literally a portal to spirit.

But with that, the mind holds its own polarity; this shouldn't come as a surprise at this point. While the mind holds consciousness which gives us access to higher dimensions, the physical attributes of the mind will try to pull us in the other direction. The ancient yogis knew this and if you've ever done a yoga teacher training, then you've heard the sutra 1.2: "yogash *chitta-vritti-nirodhah,"* which essentially means to cease the fluctuations or chatter of the mind. This is why meditation will become increasingly difficult; it takes extreme focus and practice to still the mind in order to open up the portal. That negative polarity of the mind which consists of emotions, distractions, desires, and pain, is part of the same energy that wants to keep you reincarnating—cycling through lives and never ascending. In meditation alone, we learn to combat it.

There are a few ways to meditate, but I want to talk about the difference between active and passive meditation.[17] Active meditation consciously utilizes this portal more so than your other option. With an active meditation and a little bit of training, you can call in guides, spirits, and teachers, read past lives, and perform energetic healings. This is psychic work, and by nature of being human, we all have this capability. It just depends if you want to train it up or not. On that same note, do some research on what consciousness is capable of—psychokinesis, remote viewing, using consciousness to see—we have immense power over our physical reality.

Passive meditation is most likely what you imagine when you think about meditation and what the yogis are talking about. It is the effort to still the mind, detach from thoughts, listen to the breath, and maybe even repeat a mantra.

Whichever one you do, meditation is the best tool you can have around your belt. This is how you practice sitting with yourself and truly turning inward. If you want to be on the spiritual path, meditation is your walking stick. And if you don't want to be on the spiritual path, meditation soothes anxiety, improves memory, aids depression and high blood pressure, and is basically free therapy. So, why not?

Beginner's guide to starting up a meditation practice: consistency is key. Start with five minutes every day at the same time each day. Stick with this and you will soon realize the personal benefits that a steady practice can yield. Begin to up the ante and go for ten minutes. When it feels like a chore, set a timer. There will be a shift where you might even look forward to your meditation. When this happens, leave the timer out and just go until you're done. Once you've established a routine and you stick to it, you're further along than most practitioners. You can give yourself a little more freedom in your meditation and start to explore different styles. Find a teacher. Do guided recordings. Try a past life regression meditation. Get a little freaky-deaky!

Recap. Anything that gives you insight is a tool. Our best tools will create more happiness and ease within our lives. This ease of mind mitigates the incessant babble of thoughts, anxieties, and worries, and allows us to cultivate awareness when evaluating our first nature or personal patterns. This is how we begin to do the work—by creating conscious change. We learn the lessons that we came down to learn, and in doing so, we stay on the path towards Self-realization. By continually practicing this, we embody what it means to live a spiritual existence.

This is a more modern take on the how-to behind cultivating techniques for spiritual advancement, however, it's no new-age notion. Most religions will try to teach us what it means to be a good person—the Ten Commandments for example. The betterment of the individual is a common thread throughout spirituality. We are here to be better. The core of many of our lessons lies within the foundation of simply living a moral life. You can take a look at any religious text to get ideas about what it means to be good and altruistic, but let's take a look at Buddhism.

The Noble Eightfold Path

The Buddha, in his teachings, defines the Noble Eightfold Path as the path to freeing yourself from the cycle of reincarnation and achieving liberation. The path consists of right view, right intention, right speech, right action, right livelihood, right effort, right mindfulness and right concentration. In brief, *right view* is acknowledging the universal truth that life is suffering but we can work to attain liberation from that suffering. *Right intention* means that we have the intention to do good. *Right speech* and *right action* involve saying and doing what is moral and sound. An honest acquisition of wealth is *right livelihood* and *right effort* refers to maintaining pure aspirations for both body and mind. Finally, *right mindfulness* means working towards and maintaining a productive perspective.[18]

Many religions set out to tell you how to be a faithful servant to *that* religion but the reason this Buddhist path is different is that one: it acknowledges that we all come from different circumstances, and two: it teaches the individual how to live well and do good without regard to any particular faith. It doesn't demand dependence and appears to have no hidden agenda.

Buddhism acknowledges that it isn't wise or practical for some individuals to practice renunciation—leaving their families and taking on the life of a homeless monk. He fully realized that certain circumstances give way to certain behaviors such as poverty and a higher proclivity towards theft. He didn't project shame onto those individuals but rather called for systematic changes to promote social and political stability. This was thousands of years ago and he was dropping lessons on how to deal with issues that are still a focal point in modern society. The guy was cool, man. I should also mention that there was no single Buddha. Buddha is a term that recognizes all "Perfectly Enlightened Ones" and their teachings.

Certain aspects of religious texts are amazing tools for us to use. I'm sure you've probably guessed by now that I consider Buddhist, Hindu, and Taoist teachings invaluable tools that I use to conceptualize the universe and construct my ever-evolving perspective. So, if you're someone who feels a little lost right now and not quite sure how to shed light on your lessons or how to access your spiritual path, try practicing the Eightfold

Path or any other religious or philosophical take on morality. With awareness, you'll quickly notice what is particularly hard for you and then boom—you've got yourself a lesson to work on.

No one who does good work will ever come to a bad end, either here or in the world to come.
The Bhagavad Gita

This is just one example of how you can hop into the spiritual fast-lane even if you're not quite sure where your soul fits into all this. You can slowly begin to integrate the awareness of right speech and right action into your everyday life. This alone might kickstart some incredible insight into your inner-workings. The Noble Eightfold Path is not meant to go in any particular order but instead meant to be lived all at once. Slowly start to integrate certain ideas; take what you like about it and nix what you don't. Buddha was all about modifying for your own specific life. And in today's world, I think our circumstances would call for quite a few adjustments—an ancient Buddhist would be mortified by the things we do and say on TikTok, but hey, welcome to the 21st century: era of the 12-year-old YouTube millionaire and another global pandemic.

Tools are broad in range and vary from person to person; one man's trash is another man's tool. They should initiate awareness and promote ease, but we can also use them for spiritual advancement—the quest for Self-realization. They're supposed to be helpful, so don't over complicate them. Have a few great ones on standby; these are the ones you come to again and again to promote your priorities and achieve ease of mind. Others will be used more sparingly, but with repetition, the awareness starts to bubble over the surface.

Realistically, however, we're humans and most of the time we're on autopilot. So don't turn into a psycho self-analyzer.

When something internal needs acknowledgement, it usually finds a way of coming to the surface. The real fun happens when you ignore it long enough and it begins to demand your attention in the most inconvenient ways. But don't worry, if you're using your tools and practicing awareness, you probably won't get evicted to teach you a lesson in the importance of listening to your intuition. Yeah, that was just me.

Chapter 6

Spirit Guides and Teachers

Think of a spirit as any energy that holds consciousness. Spirits exist in every realm in every dimension. In a physical realm, such as earth, we take on a physical presence; however, not all realms require embodiment. On the earthly plane, we use a human body to get around and participate; but when we're not on earth, our soul energy takes on a nonphysical presence. We are all simply energies with consciousness—the awareness of ourselves and our existence.

There is an infinite number of these energies and they all take on various roles. There are energies of a high vibration that work for the greater good and wish to help us fulfill our spiritual missions and ultimately unite with the whole-of-being. These are the lightworkers—our guides and teachers. Conversely, there are these little hellraisers of a lower vibration that ultimately work for their own more selfish intentions. They do not contribute to the greater good of humanity, and many wish to screw with us. Their energies are associated with the negative pole that wishes to keep us cycling through lives on earth—the opposite of evolution. Think of this energy as quite young and childish. They could be earthbound or visiting from another realm, but they carry with them a very mischievous energy.

Compared to that low vibrational energy, a human soul is of a more advanced frequency. It has enough sophistication to choose the path of evolution and demonstrates this by coming down to earth to live out its lessons. This flicker of our own soul deep within us yearns for our evolutionary advancement. On earth, the embodied soul depends on its spiritual connections that hold it accountable on the path to Self-realization. These are our friends, guides, and teachers—our true homies.

Because our souls long for the spirit world, it is no wonder that since the beginning of humankind, we have erected symbols and totems to recognize these otherworldly spirits guiding us here on earth. We worshipped the elements—fire and water—and then those symbols matured to individual deities within various religions. From the dawn of humanity until now, human beings, on whatever level, conscious or unconscious, have recognized these unseen energies and utilized them in order to ask for help.

Every soul has a personal guide or guides whose role it is to help that soul on its path of growth. These guides have been with us from the very beginning of our soul existence and are with us both in the soul world and in our lives on earth. You have other souls that hang around too. It's like your own personal entourage and you're Vinny Chase.

Meditation Activity

Do a quick meditation, only 5-10 minutes. Sit quietly for a few minutes focusing on your breath and deepening into the experience. Once you feel like your perception has sunken a little deeper and you're able to pull your awareness away from all external stimuli, ask your guides to step outside of the room or house for a moment. Notice any shifts. Notice how you feel without their presence around you. Then have them come back to you.[19]

Our entire life, these guides are with us. There have even been past life regression accounts of subjects under hypnosis recalling a time when they were a child and one of their guides manifested right in front of them or just as an imaginary friend.[20] The child's soul is more connected with its spirit self having had less societal and cultural influences to pull them away from their internal world. Perhaps children have a more vivid memory of the collective unconscious—another reason why our imagination is so much stronger as a child. I used to play with my dollhouses for *hours*—rearranging furniture, naming and knowing each and every one of my twenty plastic figures, forming romances between the neighborhood children, even taking them on camping trips underneath my mother's bed. Now, not even *The Sims 3* can stimulate me enough to spark that childhood passion.

If you've never felt the presence of your guides, this is a wonderful jumping-off point. From here, you can really get to know them. Call them into your meditations. Ask for a name and an image. Explore, get curious, and experiment a little bit. There are formulaic ways that were constructed by Lewis Bostwick at the Berkeley Psychic Institute, but without getting too complicated, thought drives energy. If you ask, spirit will come.

But easy does it. If you're going to play in this world, there are a few major criteria. Although spirit guides fully have your back, it's important to set your boundaries when working with these energies because not all spirit is here to serve you, and from time to time some pesky little bugger might sneak in totally in disguise. When communicating with spirit, first establish these guidelines: ensure that they serve the light, meaning they represent a helpful, high vibrational energy. Make sure they respect your time, and they come and go when asked. Request easeful communication—make sure they really vibe with you. Finally, ask that they respect your space and remind them that you, as an embodied individual, hold seniority.[21]

When you're a spirit, believe it or not, you might miss life on earth. The physical world can be very beautiful and embodiment has unique and pleasurable experiences—hello... sex! So, in a totally non-harmful way, some light-serving spirit might try to stick around and come with you to the beach. Cute, but they also know better so make sure of it by establishing these conditions.

Back to those sneaky spirits, let me clarify—just like there is energy that is good and helpful and high in frequency, the negative energy brings forth its own spirits of a lower vibration who will often have selfish motives. This is nothing to be fearful of because humans will always maintain seniority over spirit. We chose to live the embodied life which means we are here for growth. With a body comes free will so we practice a certain degree of autonomy over who can and cannot interact with us.

When I was first figuring things out in therapy, and ultimately super depressed day after day, I unintentionally met one of my guides. An obvious female presence, she came at a time where I needed to be deeply nurtured. She hung around my apartment and I sensed her with me consistently for about two months. One night while going to bed, I felt the sensation that my head was resting on a woman's lap. I could feel the physicality of her thigh underneath my cheek. It wasn't scary at all, but rather maternal. Spirit guides are looking after you, and when you need them most, they're quite close by.

I then started accessing spirit through a pendulum. All a pendulum requires is a weighted token, preferably with a pointed end, attached to a chain or piece of string. With one hand holding the top of the chain and the other making a palm about an inch or two underneath the token, say aloud that you want to communicate with your spirit guides. Have them show you a "yes," a "no," and just for good measure, a "you don't get to know that yet." You can call it a "maybe" if that's easier, but I always assume that they withhold information in order to protect your best interests. They will move the pendulum in whichever way to indicate whichever answer. (This is how I scared the shit out of that ex-boyfriend.) If you choose to try the pendulum, keep in mind that it is spirit manipulating something physical and sometimes that channel gets blocked or is misinterpreted. Use sparingly, unlike I did. I came hard and fast at my guides with all sorts of questions and found that some answers later proved to be false. I also found, however, that some of the answers they gave me shaped my perspective in a way that was necessary for me at that time, so hey—they know what they're doing.

Eventually, I started bringing in teachers. I'm a born seeker, and I want to learn as much as I can about the universe. So, who better to ask than spirit?

Back then I lacked many of the tools that I have now, but these were the first few handfuls of times that I was able to consciously connect with spirit. The female presence showed up in my life when I really needed to be taken care of; the pendulum answers made me feel less alone. When communicating with spirit, I think it's important to remember that there can never truly be any concrete answers, but from the information that you do receive from them, I bet you can intuit how it should play a role in your life.

The reason I am telling you all this is because I think that when you first start working with spirit, you're constantly doubting yourself. It's so easy to doubt what we cannot see, and although trust and faith are important qualities along this path, there is a profound impact of seeing to believe. That's why the pendulum helped me so much. By having your guides leave the room, you might feel in your physicality some anxious or unfamiliar sensation. There is comfort in evidence. As you continue along, however, you'll learn to trust yourself and your intuition and you will cultivate a tremendous amount of faith in the world around you.

Spirit is a magnificent tool where you can work in partnership with these beings. Whether or not you're cognizant of their presence, they are there with you and they want the best for you. If you choose to utilize their presence, start getting to know them. Meditate with them and talk to them. It might not be so explicit as a voice or an image popping into your head, but instead, maybe your thoughts begin to change or you might see something differently than you did before. Maybe you just *know*. In whichever way it manifests for you, this is spirit making contact. You'll definitely doubt yourself at first. I still doubt myself all the time, but definitely less than I used to.

Our Earthly Teachers

Not all our guides and teachers need to be spirits. I understand that there are some holes in the foundation when you're only relying on the voices and beings inside of your head. Mainly because the general public will call you kookie-wookie and try to institutionalize you. The ancient sages recognize that too which is why the texts offer up some wisdom about the importance of teachers—the real, human kind.

Approach those who have realized the purpose of life and question them with reverence and devotion; they will instruct you in this wisdom.

The Bhagavad Gita

Buddha devotes an entire Sutta [scripture] to describe to the monks how to tell if a teacher is good and trustworthy. Some of the criteria he lists for the monks to contemplate is whether or not this teacher practices what they preach? Do they speak and act appropriately? Have they been corrupted by attention or fame? Are they compassionate for all? The Buddha asks the monks to deliberate upon their teacher and then make their own conclusion on whether or not to award that teacher with their confidence.

This Sutta does what so many so-called teachers or gurus do not—ask the student to evaluate the teacher for authenticity. The corruption that is present throughout history in the actions and words of the "powerful teacher" is a chilling concept. Misuse of power is abominable. Manipulating someone in the position of a student is heinous. And unfortunately, it is all too prevalent in the world of spirituality. There is a difference between respect and worship. An ancient Indian guru was highly revered and respected, but he wasn't worshiped as if he were a God. And he didn't expect to be worshipped either. If you've ever watched any cult documentary or better yet, *Bikram: Yogi, Guru,*

Predator,[22] you can see firsthand how the seat of power and glorified discipleship turns a leader into a monster. Bikram was a monster, but also a complete idiot.

These are extreme examples, so let's talk about someone that I am sure you have witnessed or have come across in the wild: the pop-spiritualist. Often confined to their Instagram stories or branded partnership posts, you can sometimes spot these pop-spiritualists out in the wild teaching a class or workshop in their designated field of spirituality. Especially common in the yoga or wellness field, these guys have mad followers and a lot to say. Spirituality has somehow found itself in a weird Western pop-culture mix-up and I think that's confusing for a lot of people. In the introduction, I mentioned how a true spiritual intention has nothing to do with external validation and everything to do with inward exploration. You may have heard the saying, *"Confidence is quiet, insecurities are loud,"*[23] and it's a good rule of thumb when searching out a teacher. A good teacher is not a salesperson. They know their own abilities and trust that the student will find them. This doesn't mean that using social media to spread a message is a bad thing. Social media is a construct of our world, and oftentimes, an important part of business. It means that as students, we need to be thoughtful, diligent, and discerning. We all need a good teacher and often the best ones simply appear in our lives when we're ready to learn.

I adore my earthly teachers. One was the person who actually introduced me to this awesome world of spirit and showed me the pendulum. Another helped me continue my personal expansion and likes to nerd out over Eastern religious philosophies with me. And yet another taught me psychic techniques that ultimately broadened my perception of human limitations. Others are just authors of very important books. In their human manifestations, a teacher could be anyone: a best friend, your newborn baby, a boss. There are the ones that have studied with the masters and have acquired great wisdom or they are just regular people who enter in, with uncannily great timing, to help you realize your lessons, give you some new tool, or to nudge you back onto your path.

Keep in mind, however, that while some people might seem to serve a more important role in your evolution or personal growth, everyone you make contact with has the potential to teach you something. Hold everyone you meet in high reverence because you never know what lesson they might unveil for you unless you give them a chance.

Another final teaching from the wise and wonderful Buddha that I want to mention concerns the importance of spiritual friends. Aw Buddhy-Boi, so cute!

When a monk has a good friend, a good companion, a good comrade, it is to be expected that he will develop and cultivate the Noble Eightfold Path.
Buddha

Essentially, what Buddha is bolstering here is community. For the same reason that my friends give me that quick hit of joy, a community will care for you, hold you accountable in doing what is best for yourself, and ultimately make you feel connected. To be bound to a community is to be unconditionally supported. If you find yourself among even one or two friends who view the world the same way that you do, then consider yourself extremely lucky. As long as they are around, these friends will act as some of your greatest teachers delivering spot-on lessons right when you need them. Your individual energies have a way of weaving and jiving together in a way that supports you all at once. Just because the journey to Self-realization involves detachment from the external world and striving for personal effort, it does not mean that you have to do it alone. When you find the right friend, they support you in all your endeavors and you support them in theirs.

Chapter 7

All About Exploration

As we continue to gather our tools for awareness and joy, we can also start to figure out which tools work best for exploration — both universal and self. In Chapter 2, we discussed humanity's innate desire for concrete answers and evidence. This is true, but I've noticed that oftentimes, once we feel like we have the answers that we want and our belief system is clearly articulated, we stop exploring. We stop pushing the limits of knowledge and we fall stagnant. We opt for comfort over the discomfort that we feel from the unknown. This is where an open mind can really come into play. Exploration and discovery promotes growth and keeps you engaged while on your path. It guarantees that you push the boundaries of your belief system. As long as you explore and continue to question your surroundings — ask why — you'll never cater to anyone else's beliefs or opinions. You'll maintain your own perspective.

We've talked a lot about meditation, which we will get into a little bit more below, but there are so many other ways that we can access spirit. This next chapter will briefly describe a few techniques that I've dabbled in and will also create a good starting point for whatever piques your interest. You might find a method that resonates with you much more deeply, and if that's the case, immerse yourself in it.

The reason that I base most of this book around the spiritual texts is that they serve as ancient wisdom — tale as old as time — and the commonalities that run through the various different traditions emphasize significant elements of truth. These very same truths don't only exist in the ancient texts, however. They are repeated again and again by different sources and applications all across the spectrum providing even further evidence of this crazy universe we've got going on here. All the methods listed below are infused with spirit as long as you approach them from a spiritual perspective. Whenever we're in this mindset, positive energies will oftentimes find a way of showing you exactly what you need in whatever moment. Again, all it takes is awareness.

If you err on the more academic, black and white side of things, then look towards psychology. While much of it is still very much ingrained in the empirical, you will still come across a few psychologists who are speaking our language. Carl Jung is the most obvious example, but lots of psychologists acknowledge the importance of the subconscious, and all of them aim to help the individual become a better version of themselves.

Analytical Psychology

Carl Jung was this super heady Swiss psychologist from the late 1800s into the 1960s who founded analytical or Jungian psychology. He based his early work off of Sigmund Freud who is the founder of psychoanalysis which emphasizes the importance of both conscious and unconscious elements in the treatment of mental abnormalities. Freud, however, was a bit of a creep and Jung had other fish to fry. He separated from Freud to create his branch of psychology which utilizes aspects of religion, philosophy, anthropology, mythology, and literature. Jung believed that individuation was the human mission, meaning that our biggest priority in our personal development is to differentiate our true "Self," or soul, from our ego-self by bringing our personal and collective unconscious history into our awareness.

Jung defined the ego as our conscious mind—all the information held within our awareness. Essentially, it is what distinguishes us from animals; it is our "humanness" and represents our specific point of view. Innate in all of us is our personal unconscious and the collective unconscious. The unconscious, as you know, is a piece of our psyche that stores information of which we have no awareness, but still affects our thought processes and our behaviors. We can credit the recognition of the collective unconscious to Jung as a level of the unconscious that is shared by all of humankind. It stores our ancestral past including universal patterns and archetypes and is responsible for humankind's deeply established beliefs and instincts.[24]

Because Jung noticed all these similar themes running throughout various cultural backgrounds, he attributed these commonalities to some inborn instinct about our spiritual past stemming from this place of the collective unconscious buried deep within our psyches. In the world of psychology, much of Jung's work is dismissed due to a lack of empirical evidence. Jung did a lot of self-work and described it in mass amounts of detail. Science stops when facts end, so in a scientific world it takes much more evidence than personal experience to have your findings acknowledged; this was Jung's dilemma. His true proponents are the ones who, too, put in the same self-discipline and sought after their own answers. They know the validity of his work through personal experience.

Humanistic Psychology

If even Jung's theory of psychology is *still* too unconventional, then let's take a look at Abraham Maslow. Maslow gets a little more respect in the scientific world. A major player in the development of humanistic psychology and the creator of "Maslow's Hierarchy of Needs," Maslow too revered the human pursuit of Self-realization. Briefly, his pyramid model for human needs and desires in ascending order goes as follows: the primary needs making up the foundation of the pyramid are *physiological needs* like food, water, air, and shelter. Next is *safety* in regard to financial and personal security followed by needs concerning *love and belonging*. This includes someone's sense of connection to friends, family, and community. The desire for confidence, recognition, and freedom makes up the level of *esteem*, and finally, at the very top, once all other needs are met is *Self-actualization*.[25]

Maslow believed in human potential—that we have power over our decision making and that those decisions push us down our path towards personal growth. Although it's not the best psychological approach for severe mental illnesses, if you're just a regular old joe with a touch of anxiety here, maybe a tidbit of mania there, certainly a bout of depression every once in a while, then the humanistic approach is very useful. It helps us very clearly define our priorities. One of my teachers always says, *"You can't meditate in a house on fire,"* and I think that's useful advice here. It means start with the basics—food, water, shelter—and then climb your way up the pyramid. You certainly cannot attain Self-realization if you're starving, or you hate yourself, or you have no sense of community, or your house is on fire.[26]

If you're not one to respond to past lives and the idea of the collective unconscious, then read up on the humanistic approach to psychology or better yet find a dope therapist that takes insurance. But really, all of us should take a page out of the ole Maslow Handbook. It's important to know and understand our needs so that we can learn how to properly nourish ourselves.

Past Life Regression

Because we've already gone over past life regression, thanks to the wisdom of the sexiest past life regressionist around, I'll keep this section brief. There are many psychologists out there like Michael Newton, who have contributed to the growing research coming out of hypnotherapy case studies. All of these practitioners are totally credited and have simply crossed the line between the empirical and the abstract. Not only has this method opened up doors into the soul world and past lives, but we have learned about Atlantis, extraterrestrials, subjects jumping forward on the linear timeline into future lives, the confirmation of mythical beasts like Bigfoot and the Loch Ness Monster, and so, so much more. Upon reading these accounts, you realize that myth, legends, and folklore might very well be long continuations of oral tradition passed down from our eldest ancestors or perhaps simply memories stored in the collective unconscious. The information coming through from these hypnotherapy sessions might seem bizarre or extreme in nature but also goes to show that this universe is beyond bigger than we could ever imagine.

If you're lucky, you might have a past life regressionist in your town. If so, do your due diligence and make sure that they're legitimate before coughing up hundreds of dollars. Another option is past life regression meditation recordings—search Brian Weiss and try his videos out.

Myth

While on the topic of mythical beings, if you're more of a fantastical, whimsical, or creative person, perhaps myth is your doorway. As previously mentioned, many myths are believed to be expressions of the collective unconscious making it even less of a coincidence that many of the same stories and characters are found within the folklores of cultures with no history of interaction.

Think of the Odyssey—the epic Hero's Journey. This paradigm is one of man's oldest archetypal storylines: a long journey home filled with twists and turns, obstacles, and tests. Like any archetypal definition—I'm right there with C.J.—I truly believe that it stems from somewhere within our deep psyche out of the collective unconscious and represents our soul's true instinctual nature to return back to the source from which we came. Stories are powerful because they speak to our inner nature and evoke emotional responses.

Clarissa Pinkola Estés, author of *Women Who Run with the Wolves*, can probably say it better than anyone, so I'll turn it over to her:

Stories are medicine... They have such power; they do not require that we do, be, act anything—we need only listen. The remedies for repair or reclamation of any lost psychic drive are contained in stories. Stories engender excitement, sadness, questions, longings, and understandings that spontaneously bring the archetype... back to the surface. Stories are embedded with instructions which guide us about the complexities of life.

We know this. We've all pored over novels and short stories in academic settings and have written pages of essays explicating the way this author or that book was able to convey a lesson that is not only powerful, but universal. We look towards the myths and the folklore for the root of these lessons. They are the earliest adaptations of archetypes and patterns, and they're told in ways to help the listener navigate life. If you read them with awareness and apply the lessons to your own circumstances, then you can most definitely claim the path of Self-realization.

Accessing the Superconscious State

Both meditation and breathwork, along with various other practices, are our gateways into the superconscious state. Both of these practices are two of the oldest tricks in the book and have been used by all the greatest yogis for thousands of years. If you recall, the superconscious is that deeply rooted core of the psyche that connects you with the spiritual realm or the seat of your Higher Self.

The superconscious has many levels. When you start to feel an element of calm, you have penetrated the surface of the superconscious and you can begin to move towards a higher frequency as you access feelings of tranquility, bliss, love, and peace. For many, this is the source of profound creativity. At the most extreme level of this state, one feels a total merge with universal consciousness. Just for fun, let's read a passage from *Autobiography of a Yogi*, where Yogananda explains his first experience accessing the deepest levels of the superconscious:

> *An oceanic joy broke upon calm endless shores of my soul. The Spirit of God, I realized, is exhaustless Bliss; His body is countless tissues of light. A swelling glory within me began to envelop towns, continents, the earth, solar and stellar systems, tenuous nebulae, and floating universes. The entire cosmos, gently luminous, like a city seen afar at night, glimmered within the infinitude of my being. The sharply etched global outlines faded somewhat at the farthest edges; there I could see a mellow radiance, ever-undiminished. It was indescribably subtle; the planetary pictures were formed of a grosser light.*
>
> *The divine dispersion of rays poured from an Eternal Source, blazing into galaxies, transfigured with ineffable auras. Again and again I saw the creative beams condense into constellations, then resolve into sheets of transparent flame. By rhythmic reversion, sextillion worlds passed into diaphanous luster; fire became firmament.*
>
> *I cognized the center of the empyrean as a point of intuitive perception in my heart. Irradiating splendor issued from my nucleus to every part of the universal structure. Blissful amrita, the nectar of immortality, pulsed through me with a quicksilverlike fluidity. The creative voice of God I heard resounding as Aum, the vibration of the Cosmic Motor.*

Um, sure. Twist my arm. I'll give meditation a shot. For many of these techniques, I recommend taking a class or finding a guide before you do it by yourself. There are various breathwork techniques—you may have heard of holotropic, which involves fast-paced rhythmic breathing. It's essentially self-induced hyperventilation and makes for a very wild experience. As far as meditation, there are hundreds of different "types." I explained how to start up your own meditation practice in Chapter 5, but if you feel like you need more guidance, find a class or do guided meditations on the Headspace or Insight Timer apps.

Divination

In some of the more trendy spirituality circles, it can be très chic to call yourself a witch. So if you're feeling rather witchy, you might like divination. To be fair, there are plenty of actual witches and—wizards? warlocks? whatever the male equivalent is—but you can tell the real ones from the fake ones because the real ones don't give a shit about looks and the fake ones, oddly enough, really do. The real ones also do real magick.[27]

All divination means is communing with the divine in order to uncover knowledge about the future or the unknown, so really, it's right up our alley. Again, this is something that is used in Occultism, so naturally, Satan's involved. Right? Now I should explain Occultism, which really is just a broad term involving beliefs or practices pertaining to the supernatural, mystical, and magickal. Like anything, Occultism can be used to access either the dark or the light, but we're in it for the light and Satan isn't allowed.

Divination tools include the pendulum, tarot cards, tea readings, herbs, oils, and crystals. My favorite divination tool is the *I Ching*, an ancient Chinese text used within Buddhist, Confucian and Taoist traditions. Each of its 64 hexagrams shed light on some universal truth and are used to help guide its seekers toward moral decision making.

Astral Projection

Astral projection is a way to explore the astral realm using your subtle or etheric body. For most, it is a very hard practice to develop, but with time and dedication, I definitely think it's possible for anyone who's committed. This can happen when one reaches a meditative or sleeplike state where the physical body is checked out, but the mind is alert and conscious. From here, you reach a vibratory state that can elicit the detachment of your subtle body from your physical body. If you've ever heard of an out-of-body or near-death experience, where someone recounts floating over their physical body from above, it's similar in nature.

During these experiences, you might simply stay in the same area of your physical body or you might travel somewhere on earth or within the astral. With practice, you can visit places in the astral realm such as healing temples or the Akashic Records. I recommend getting some books and doing some research, but if this is something you can master then I think that is a very cool thing.

Psychedelics

I had to throw them in here because when used responsibly and as a tool, these little puppies can do some serious work. My psychedelic of choice are psilocybin mushrooms, but ayahuasca, LSD and DMT are some other potent variables among others. Psychedelics are sometimes referred to as shortcuts because they allow you access to the superconscious and other realms of thought without much effort, but I think that if they allow you insight into your personal path, then what's the difference?

Again, this is another thing that I don't recommend doing alone if it's your first time. If you're serious about using these substances to enhance your personal understanding, then it might be worth it to find a guide to lead you through the journey. The dosage depends on what you're comfortable with, but better to start small and work your way up. The levels of intensity vary from trip to trip and the most important thing to consider is set and setting. Make sure that you're in a good headspace and take them in a place where you feel comfortable.

Luckily for us, by nature of being a human, and thus a microcosm of the entire universe, we already have all the knowledge within us. We use the tools listed above to help us see the way, to know what to look for, and to uncover the truths within. Tools are helpful, but ultimately it's the inward trajectory that leads to the most thrilling explorations. Take it from one of my favorite chapters of the *Tao Te Ching*:

> *Without going outside, you may know the whole world.*
> *Without looking through the window, you may see the ways of heaven.*
> *The farther you go, the less you know.*
>
> *Thus the wise know without traveling;*
> *See without looking;*
> *Work without doing.*
> Tao Te Ching, Ch. 47

As you continue down your path of effort, growth, and truth, the twists and turns will lead you to certain people, places and sources that will further inform whatever trajectory you have chosen. That's just another way that the universe unfolds for us. So again, begin with whatever resonates and do research, talk to people, and most importantly try new things — even if they scare you a little bit. That's where growth happens. Wherever you are right now, take a look back a few years and notice how and why every person, place, and thing that crossed your path ultimately helped guide your mission to where you are now. If the answers aren't quite clear, give it a little more time.

Chapter 8

The Ego-Principle

For our last chapter in Part Two, we must define the ego—man's greatest foe! When we think of the ego, our minds think of self-obsession and suddenly jump to that egotistical, arrogant asshole boss or coworker or dude you met at a party in West Hollywood that one time, but in actuality, the ego-principle can be much more subtle than that.

First, let's differentiate between Jung's ego and the ego-principle of Eastern theology. As mentioned previously, Jung defines the ego as the essence inside all of us that makes us uniquely human. It's a part of the mind that reflects our consciousness or how we perceive ourselves based on the known information. It does not include all that is unconscious. In Jung's perception, the ego is a neutral force innate in every human being. This isn't the real enemy.

In Eastern tradition, the ego is responsible for the separation between humankind and the Creator Source. The ego illuminates upon our differences whether it be class, culture, goals, desires, beliefs, likes, or dislikes. It creates an "us versus them" dynamic and leads to further divide. This force within us is so inherent that we hardly even realize when it activates, nor do we realize the incessancy of its impact. As a tier of energy working for the negative force, the ego will try to enchant you into believing that you are separate from everyone else. We know this is false because we know our history. We all emanate from "the One" where we are of the same caliber. It's delusion to believe anything different, but because the notion of separateness is so present in the modern world, we're often blind to the ego's strength.

I am constantly comparing myself to others, and whether

it's driven by competition or self-loathing these thoughts cycle through my mind with little to no warning and vary from the petty to the extreme. On the side of pettiness, I am constantly catching myself comparing my body to other women. The essence of comparison is the undertone of separation. On the other end of that spectrum, when I feel a sense of superiority or advantage for the beliefs that I hold, I know that I am letting my ego run the game. For the majority of my life, this force has been operating on autopilot running continuous cycles of ego-driven thought without my awareness. This is one of humanity's biggest dangers. If we let our egos run unchecked, then we continue to grow more and more separate, and we allow man and creator to further polarize.

The Veil of Maya

The ego operates under the Veil of Maya. All this talk about the negative energy, well, this is the term for it—a concept stemming from Eastern theology referring to delusion.[28] The history of maya began with the Fall of Man—not to be confused with Christianity's interpretation. From my understanding, The Fall was a real event that took place in our very faraway past. Religions have distorted what may have actually occurred, but the overarching idea is that this is the episode where something went wrong and the negative forces came down to rule over the lower three realms.

We'll save the details, however, for another book. All we need to know right now is that on earth, maya is extremely present but very well concealed. It is a force that masks our infinite and limitless reality by making us believe that the world around us is actually finite and limited. The reality that we know is ruled by Time and Space—two constructs that create separateness between us. Time tells us that our lives are limited, that our history is linear, and that along this linear line, there is a beginning and an end. Space tells us that we are of this single earthly plane and blinds us to the implicit actualities of what goes on beyond our perceivable vision.

When the veil is lifted, time is not linear but happening all at once. Time exists simultaneously where through our consciousness we can access what we understand to be the past, present, or future. Other areas of Space are accessible too, through consciousness. We can explore other realms or discover entryways into parallel universes. When the veil is lifted, we break through the barriers of our limited perceptions illustrated to us by our minds. We achieve a "higher state" where we recognize the inseparable whole.

As humans living on earth, we define ourselves by our limits and we sense division among mankind. We're prone to differentiating the world into categories and schema in order to help ourselves understand what's going on but ultimately this blinds us to the truth of the big picture. Buddhist and Hindu texts teach us that in order to become free, we must rid ourselves of the aspect of the ego that promotes separateness in order to lift the veil. This doesn't mean that we surrender our personalities and our defining attributes, but rather we recognize and abandon these "ego-thoughts" that attempt to create the separate notion of us and them.

So what fuels the ego and how can we lessen its burn? In a broad overview, the answer has to do with self-satisfaction through attachments and desires—but let's clarify that. Attachments and desires can manifest within physical objects but also through thoughts and perceptions. And don't get me wrong, it's okay to want things—that's what drives motivation and encourages growth. For example, we must allow ourselves to desire Self-realization, otherwise, no one would set forth on the path. The difference is that we must practice releasing the desire for any particular outcome. Everything you do should be fueled by making the decision that is right for yourself, but not by any attachment to an outcome that it might yield. I practice meditation daily. Of course, my hope is that through this practice I might gain some form of information or insight every time I meditate, but that is not always the case. I can't get pissed if nothing comes through. I meditate knowing that it is the right thing for me, but I release any expectation of the positive outcome. In meditation or in life, we will yield both good and bad results, and every time our job is to maintain a sense of neutrality despite a positive or negative outcome.

When we attach, it's our ego talking. We believe that the object of our attachment defines who we are whether it be a Toyota Forerunner, an executive position at Google, wanting to be perceived as intelligent or easygoing or a hardass—these are all external validations fueled by the ego. By releasing attachments, we allow the soul, driven purely by selfless motivations, to work through us.

When I moved from my sweet little apartment in Santa Monica, I ultimately decided it wasn't worth it to pack a moving truck for all my home decor, plants, and furniture—most of it collected in back alleyways, but loved nonetheless. Honestly, I was fairly obsessed with the belongings I had acquired. My fiddle leaf fig had nearly doubled in size and I had an amazing San Pedro cactus that was hard to come by. I thought I was some kind of nonattachment goddess when I simply decided to let it all go, but now I realize that the relinquishment of material things— most often attributed to the concept of nonattachment—is not what is so difficult about this practice. The true effort that lies behind releasing attachments and desires comes with a total restructuring and training of the mind. Material things are easy to point to and say, "Release!" The hard stuff to release involves our preconceived notions, our beliefs, and our fears— the mental stuff, man. The underlying mental stuff drives our motives so the true task is distinguishing selfish motives versus selfless motives.

Selfless motives are cool. That's not what's feeding this hungry little monster that we call ego. We must be wary of the selfish attachments. In order to get really good at discerning your underlying motives, ask yourself the true intention behind any word, thought, or action, and if it fuels the ego or if it boosts your own sense of personal worth by creating division then you best check yourself, brah. Universal example: we all talk shit about people. Why though? To make ourselves feel better? To entertain our friends? To blend in with the crowd? It's so common but rarely do we ask ourselves the underlying intention and rarely do we realize that it is totally ego-driven. We need a new technique. Perhaps respectful venting? It's still venting but at least it's done with the acknowledgement of the other person's side of the story.

Quite frankly, many of us won't rid ourselves of the ego and obtain a perfect union with Source *in this lifetime,* but luckily for us, Self-realization carries over. Any work you achieve in this life in subduing your ego will give you a leg up in the next life.

The ego inherits the mind and drives humanity apart. The soul is immune to the ego and is totally motivated by the collective achievement of humanity as a whole. The more we are able to realize the presence of the ego and the more we are able to access the soul through our human formations, the easier we can mitigate this divisive force within ourselves and within our earthly communities.

Once again, the path is not austere. It's pliable and conducive towards your efforts. Always, always, always, start with awareness. Notice your desires, your wants, and your needs. Then, begin to uncover the underlying intention and the hoped-for result. Is it me-driven? Does it create a divide? The next step is to let the outcome go. Disengage. Practice a sense of neutrality and control over the mind. It's okay to strive for things, but don't let your perception of the result get inside your head. Of all the negative forces trying to keep you reincarnating, the ego is supreme. The distraction that it creates completely undermines the actual reason behind our existence—that we are separate when we are actually whole, that selfishly desiring will somehow make you "better than."

The ego wants to prevent your evolution. No matter where you are on your path to Self-realization or even just your path to becoming a better person, controlling the ego will give you a sense of personal freedom and collective unity. It gets us a little closer to that infinite and limitless soul-space that we call home.

Actionless Action

When we are able to attain the "egoless" state, we achieve this idea of actionless action. The ego-force is externally driven, but when one is occupying the seat of their soul—letting their soul enact through them unperturbed by ego-influence—they are able to act from a place that is completely internal and collectively bound. It's the Source or God-energy flowing through the human being. It's a hard state to achieve and an even harder state to maintain, but its biggest characteristic is the absence of the pitfalls of ego. Rather than thinking, "I am separate from my soul," it's believing that, "I am a vessel for my soul." When we let the Soul act through us, we are performing our greatest work and it has nothing to do with slapping your name on it.

A person who acknowledges this state does their work for the collective, completely void of selfish attachments and ego. Internally, they are at ease having freed themselves from the delusion of separation. Outwardly, they see the entire picture. A person in a state of actionless action sees the world through the soul and acts on behalf of others rather than themselves.

Competing with no one, they are alike in success and failure and content with whatever comes to them. They are free, without selfish attachments; their minds are fixed in knowledge. They perform all work in the spirit of service, and their karma is resolved.

The Bhagavad Gita

The Gita acknowledges that by having a human body, there is just no such thing as inaction. The point of living an embodied existence is because it gives us the physicality to actually perform work on earth. A monk undergoes renunciation when he gives up all his earthly belongings, but *The Gita* tells us that true renunciation has little to do with material belongings and more to do with the renunciation of desires. Easier said than done, I know. Many of us have no idea what our soul's will is, but we're starting to get a feel for what is right and wrong. Start here. In this microcosm, infuse every day with awareness and choose to do the right thing versus the wrong thing. If you start to get a feel for your soul's vocation, let everything you do be in service to that mission.

I want to reiterate something here. The world we see in front of us is messy and our goal is to try to approach it from a place of understanding. This does not mean, however, that we need to be complaisant. Just as Arjuna had a duty to lead his people into war, we too have certain duties that we must fulfill. I am by no means promoting violence, but I want to ensure that we're on the same page. Sometimes harsh actions, like Arjuna's war, are actually warranted as long as they are backed by intentions rooted in morality and doing the right thing. It gets a little complicated by the fact that morality and ethics are hotly debated and there will always be someone whose sense of right and wrong is different from yours. I get frustrated by this every day. Humanity is frustrating. Educate and inform others whenever you can, but know that some people just won't hear you. Do what is right for you and choose your battles *wisely*. Trust that those on the opposing side will one day learn their lessons and know that it's not your job to change them. That's all I am going to say about that.

All of us have innate soul-desires that are selflessly constructed. Maybe your soul came down to realize some personal lessons; maybe you're here for someone else; maybe you're here to create change or growth in your local community; maybe you're here to heal others; whatever it is, this is your vocation—the action your soul wishes to perform in this lifetime.

The more this vocation comes into view, the more you want to focus all your energy on the mission, and the less you want to do *literally* anything else. This is a common pitfall, and so the sages acknowledge it:

The soul must stretch over the cosmogonic abysses, while the body performs its daily duties.

Paramahansa Yogananda

Our practice is to continually realize the efforts of our soul while our human body takes care of its responsibilities. Paying your bills allows you to live in a house where you can peacefully meditate. Do you see what I mean? Even the mundane actions of embodiment can be in service to the soul; you just have to see it that way.

This is all connected to the ego because the ego plays a major role in whether or not we are able to acknowledge our soul's will. If we diminish the ego and practice humility, our soul shines through and we can realize the mission. We then act for each other rather than ourselves. By the soul initiating this action, the human remains actionless and at ease. It is the effortless effort behind letting our soul call the shots.

Someone very wise once gave me some life advice. He said, *"Every day, practice gratitude, humility, and meditation."* To me, that's how you feed the soul and diminish the ego. That's how we create the space for the soul to work through us. It also goes to show that simplicity in perspective can teach the greatest lessons.

What we've just looked at is the core of the ego in the realm of Buddhist and Hindu theology, and it's prevalent information for those of us on our paths. But to sum it all up neatly, we all know what it means to be egotistical. We've all encountered it and we've all demonstrated it ourselves, if not outwardly, definitely in our thoughts. It's a product of being a human living on planet earth. The intention behind every thought, word, or deed will let you know if the ego is trying to take control. If the intention is selfish or drives external desires and leads to separateness, the ego is trying to take the wheel. If the intention is pure and selfless, however, then the ego is in the back seat where it belongs.

Whether or not you want to apply the principles talked about in this chapter, it all comes back to understanding.

The ego wants to divide us, and the nature of understanding works to connect us together. It's another dualistic force that we can mediate. As you continue your own self-work, self-understanding, and Self-realization, you might at times feel like you have the answers and the puzzle is beginning to piece itself together. Be wary of this trap. If you're reading this book, then it seems like Self-realization and this idea of personal effort is something that you prioritize. Not everyone will see the merit in it and that's fine. They're no worse, you're no better. The longer we start uncovering the mysteries of the universe and ourselves the more we will realize that we know absolutely nothing. Don't let the ego make you think otherwise.

I'm just going to say it—the ego is a dick. He inserts himself into our mind and controls our thoughts, all without consent I might add. But the empowering thing behind his troublesome existence is that we can control him. In fact, it's part of the human mission to quiet his relentless cries. And we have a lot of tools to do so. Awareness is key in determining our attachments and desires, and the premise behind actionless action gives us a tangible starting point to infuse into our day or our overall life mission. We can subdue this little guy as long as we acknowledge his worthless nature.

To-Ponder List

Awareness is everything in the acknowledgement of who you actually are. We're often blind to the energies that come into contact with us. We don't recognize our guides' subtle cueings. We're inattentive to our intuition, our patterns and our lessons. Have you heard of the Baader-Meinhof phenomenon? Essentially, it's when you become aware of something that seems new, and all of a sudden you notice it popping up everywhere. Spiritual awareness is a little bit like that. Once you become aware of some new pattern, the information will come pouring in. Although unlike the Baader-Meinhof phenomenon, this isn't an illusion. It will just feel that way.

- **Have you ever had a past life experience, vision, or intuitive feeling?** Do you have any, what seem like random, reactions, emotions, or fears that arise out of nowhere traceable?
- **What do you dream about?** Do you experience recurring people or places?
- **What are your personal patterns?** What thoughts, emotions or behaviors do you often exhibit without thinking? Which ones do you like? Which ones do you not like?
- **What activities or hobbies do you do the most often?** How do you do them? Do you rush through them or perform them very meticulously? Do you do it with others or alone? Do they bring up any emotions? Do they feel worthwhile? Do they feel like a chore? Are they fun? Compare the way you do one activity to the way you do another. Are there any patterns?
- **List your tools for joy.**
- **Give me a few quick hits.**
- **Who have been your greatest teachers?** What have they

taught you?

- **Are you interested in exploration?** Does it scare you? Will you consider any of the exploration tools from the previous section?

Part Three

Chapter 9

Big Picture Thinking

Wow, we're here. We've worked our way through a lot of intricate concepts—reading and comprehension are one thing, but the actual integration of these ideas is a lifelong task.

This next section is devoted to looking at the big picture and what that means in navigating your own life. Then we'll tie it all up in a big bow and march off together into the world spiritual guns blazin'.

Big picture thinking is another term that brings us back to the idea of perspective. Remember those reel viewer toys from the 90s? You'd insert a round reel, look through a set of plastic binoculars, and click the lever on the side to switch to the next picture. This is how I imagine perspective. You get to choose through which lens you want to view the world. You can view it from a "me-informed" ego space; through the lens of the collective; zoomed in or zoomed out. Each view or lens has its own set of constructs and limitations—a set of rules—that vary from slide to slide. Big picture thinking is just one of the slides on the reel that you can click to in your mind; it's a frame of reference. It's taking all that we know about the inner workings of the universe and pasting it over your life so that you can more easily see the patterns.

As a soul embodied, one that is walking the path of Self-realization, you're constantly in flux between your human, earthly state and your soul state. Because we err on what is familiar, we more often see the world through our human eyes— finite and limited. It takes much more effort to "bounce up" a level and see the world through an elevated perspective.

Metaphorical Analysis Alert!

Imagine that you are climbing a mountain. You start at basecamp and start hiking one foot in front of the other. You can see the path immediately in front of you and immediately behind you, but otherwise, the trees are tall and the cliffs are massive and everything ahead of you obscures your view. This is the path of perspective. As a human, you'll always be able to see and know what's going on around you by your limited radius and you will use that information to guide your thoughts, words, and actions. As you climb higher, however, you're able to see more and your perspective widens. The more path that you have behind you, the more you're able to see how all the pieces inevitably fit into the whole.

At the summit, you look out and see 360° around you, the entire picture. You watch the seasons change and they help orient you in your own season of life. Day and night come by and tell you about the ebb and flow of ease and hardship. The sun reminds you of a deeply rooted purpose to return home. At the top of the mountain, you might use this vantage point to take a deep breath and realize the fine orchestration behind existence—that everything will be okay.

Coming back to the big picture reminds us as humans of the greater plan. It reminds us of our true nature of souls on a playground doing our best to learn and grow—that nothing should be taken too seriously. This is the essence of big picture thinking, but it is not our natural state of mind. As humans, most of us have always seen the world through the eyes of the human. It takes a lot of work and awareness to shift into this gear of the big picture, to break the limits of time and space, and to trust in the unknown.

As we discover our lessons on earth and continue efforting through personal work, we sometimes get caught up in this "ground-level," earthly perspective and life feels a little overwhelming. Our first job is to catch it as early as we can, and from there, we reframe what is really going on.

It sounds easy enough, but when we're down there, toiling through the mud, it can be hard to notice that we've gotten sucked into this ground-level state of mind. The more we're on this level, the farther we remove ourselves from our summit perspective and we get caught up in fear, anxiety, and doubt—all of whom work very hard to cloud our perspective. With practice, however, it gets easier and easier to bounce up.

Family for me is a huge source of ground-level thinking— one that reappears often and never fails to crush my spirits and leave me spiteful towards them and loathing for myself. This is how I reframe it: for whatever reason, my soul chose this life. Personally, I think he's into pushing boundaries.[29] Every negative narrative that I have created for myself due to my upbringing is a part of my lessons and my work is to rewrite the narrative. The people who have disappointed me—or rather, their souls— actually have my greatest interests in mind and care deeply for me. I sometimes long for the sense of family, but that's because I have known it well in other lives and this life is about something different. I love them for being my teachers and the instigators of my growth.

This is how I personally teach myself to perceive my family. And it's so funny because even writing this, in my head, no matter how much work I've put towards this, there is still a deep, scratchy little monster voice that says, "They ruined you," and then goes on to bite off the head of a tiny forest creature. It's all just proof that big picture thinking is a hard thing to integrate into your understanding no matter how much time you spend climbing that mountain.

Yes, we can all step back and acknowledge the big picture, but it's an entirely different thing to believe it day in and day out. You will get sucked back down towards the earthly perspective, there's no doubt. But the true art is in the reverberation[30]—how quickly can you get yourself back up the mountain and see the bigger picture.

Earth versus soul thinking is one of the most critical changes of perspective that we can give ourselves. The human and the soul create a partnership once the two link up at birth, but at certain points we must begin to separate our "humanness" from our soul in order to distinguish between the two. The human being, after all, is really just a creature without its soul. The body is the vehicle that we use in order to operate on earth and it functions beneath the laws of nature. With the soul, however, we have a purpose that stems from a higher source and we can access intelligence and wisdom from the higher realms. When we get too caught up in our "humanness," we're giving in to the forces of distraction. Utilize the human body, treat it well and have fun with it, but your true work lies with the soul and the soul sees the world from the top of the mountain.

In all the previous chapters, we've touched on some aspect of big picture thinking. All of them can be applied to help you control your direction and rein in your perspective, but here are a few more examples that we can use.

Fundamental Laws of the Universe

Fundamental laws are just that—fundamental. They create the structure by which the universe operates and therefore can be applied directly to your life. For example, let's look at the Law of Karma which essentially states that everything that happens to us is some result of something that we have previously done. Therefore any action, physical or mental, acts as both a cause and an effect. It's said that we continue incarnating until all our karma is worked out between every soul that we've ever made contact with. This is the reason that we continue reincarnating with those primary, secondary, and probably tertiary groups of souls. Every thought, word, or deed, good or bad, will ultimately get shot out into the universe and at some point in time come back down to affect us whether it be in this life or another life to come.

Big picture thinking, with regards to the Law of Karma, means do good as often as you can, because the bad will sneak up on you and mess you up. But hey, let's face it. All of us in our past lives have probably committed some sort of horrendous evil. So in this life, whenever the bad happens—tiny nuisances or major tragedy—know that it is your karma being worked out on the cosmic scale. Remember that life is not finite and nothing is such a huge deal that you won't be able to recover from it. Then, whenever that bad thing is over—because it will be over—give yourself a sigh of relief because you got that karma out of the way. You survived it. One of my teachers once told me that two of the biggest ways that you might repay karma are through illness or large financial payments. I've had to fork over so much cash in this life, but jokes on them, because I know that I'm just slam-dunking my karmic debt left and right.

Universal Pattern

One universal pattern that I've been using a lot lately is the Vedic Trinity: create, sustain, destroy, depicted by Brahma, Vishnu, and Shiva. This concept is a universal pattern that relays the three forces of God or the universe and can be seen in every facet of our lives. It's the essence of a cycle. In 2020, the world has been looking a little dreary—okay it's been looking unbelievably ominous. When I am in the depths of my ground-level perspective, I lose all faith in humanity and I want to give up—take me home! But when I am able to bounce up and broaden my perspective, I look at this pattern. I believe that we're in the destruction phase. Humanity was created. We wandered, we domesticized, we industrialized, we philosophized, we studied, we engineered, we populated the planet, we overpopulated the planet, we took advantage of our resources, we got greedy and corrupted. Here we are now. Our planet is wrecked, our country needs a leader, and humanity, as a whole, looks like it's on its way out. But, what we are seeing emerging is certain groups of people rising up to create change. Old and outdated systems are shaking in their boots. We're at a turning point.

Change is on the horizon, but will it be integral and impactful? Destruction sounds scary, but it's the same reason that a farmer burns her crop fields at the end of harvest—to create a new beginning for the Spring. This universal pattern is also present in your life. No matter the scale, how many times has something good followed something tremendously bad? For me, every time. Change creates growth. It gives us an opportunity to level up and the knowledge of this pattern is just enough to help get us through the woods when destruction comes around.

The Number Three

I love these numbers. Sacred geometry is the most principal construct of the cosmos—the universal language. We discussed the numbers one through three. One implies the universal motion of equal expansion and movement back towards center. This is our soul's direction. Two is duality; the idea that everything is created in opposition to something else. And three mediates opposition in order to strike balance.

In this example, you get to be the mediator. You're always working between two opposite forces: hot and cold; lazy and energized; depression and elation; effort and grace. This last one can be tremendously helpful for us. We're continuously moderating how much effort we put forth and how much grace we allow. Think of a workaholic: The stereotype of a workaholic is someone who incessantly works and never takes a break. This person is awesome at efforting but horrible at grace. Now think of a beach bum—great at grace, not so great with effort. We need to strike our own personal balance between dual forces—personal because it is unique to you and applies to your circumstances. If you work four hours a day, but those four hours require mass amounts of effort and energy then don't compare yourself to someone who works eight hours a day but gabs at the water cooler for half of it. Effort gets us what we want and grace allows us to actually enjoy the things we want.

Take comfort that when you exert effort, grace will come in one way or another. But here's the catch: try not to expect grace. If you recall, to expect a certain outcome is to desire and attach. Trust that grace will come, but don't expect it because you believe that it is deserved. Here's what The Gita tells us:

You have the right to work, but never to the fruit of work. You should never engage in action for the sake of reward, nor should you long for inaction. Perform work in this world... without selfish attachments, and alike in success and defeat. For yoga is perfect evenness of mind.
The Bhagavad Gita

Everything we do is about moderation and balance. The universe seeks balance in every action or event that takes place, therefore, as humans we learn from this divine reciprocity. Notice when you resort to extremes and then consciously effort towards your own middle. This is the essence of the number three.

Archetypes

Archetypes help us to categorize our surroundings so that we can understand more complex personalities, motives, and behaviors. Archetypes are like the prototypes—the very first idea of something that has been replicated many times across many mediums. They can be people, patterns, or ideas and they're inbred in all of us making them universal concepts.

Much of our external world can be divided up into relative archetypes that help us gain access to the core of their meaning. For example, let's take a look at one of Jung's archetypes: the child and more specifically, "the wounded inner-child." This archetype exists in all of us to a varying degree. The child deals with our deeply rooted yearning for the naivety and innocence of our childhoods. The wounded inner child archetype is the piece of you that might feel neglected and betrayed and accompanies the awareness of our upbringing under the lens of a more mature and refined adult perspective. If you've ever mourned for your younger self, this is that archetype manifesting in your cognitive awareness.

Another primitive example is the archetype of male and female. Don't get too distracted by male and female as representations of a gender, however. These attributes are solely in essence, simply semantics, and if you get caught up in gender roles, you might miss the bigger picture. In Taoism, yin symbolizes the female and yang symbolizes the male. Yin represents elements like receptivity, nurture, emotions, intuition, patience, and passivity—qualities that are female in nature. Yang includes elements like heat, vigor, activity, logic, passion, and strength—qualities that are considered masculine. We all embody qualities on both sides and, while it has a little to do with whether you are a male or a female, it is more about striking a balance between these two oppositional forces.

We all embody qualities that are both male and female, and many of us lean more to one side or the other having nothing to do with our physical gender. Like everything that we do, we can work to find a balance of masculine and feminine within ourselves. Jung had an archetype for this: the anima or the animus, which is the unconscious feminine in males and the unconscious masculine in females. We can also call this the divine male and the divine female. If we see a leader who embodies the characteristic of being strong and firm while at the same time gentle and patient, this person has struck a nice balance between their divine inner male and female.

On the big picture level, archetypes can not only define ourselves and our current situation but also work to define global or universal patterns. On earth, presently, we are in a phase that is driven by the masculine and ruled by the patriarchy. At one point or another, on earth, the feminine ruled and the female form was worshipped. These both, however, are two extremes. Just like the strong and gentle leader, humanity needs to work towards a place where the divine masculine and the divine feminine unite in order to restore a place of balance— characterized by both integrity and peace. We want this on the universal level of course, but that will only change once we achieve it on the human level. We must all strive to strike this balance within ourselves and allow that balance to carry itself out into the world.

Archetypes contribute to big picture thinking by indicating the type of person or situation that surrounds you, the unconscious reasons beneath certain desires, as well as the larger scale universal map of what is really going on. If you were to write your story into a fairytale, these people, places, and ideas create the underlying symbolism to conceptualize your narrative from a more universal and symbolic viewpoint.

Like our chapter on exploration and the various different portals to knowledge, all of these examples represent different tools to gain a summit-perspective. You'll realize what works best for you and you'll start to discover more ways in which that particular lens might aid your understanding. Whenever I take psilocybin mushrooms, I always go in with questions regarding my earthly, present, here-and-now concerns and I always come back with a newfound understanding of universal pattern. Surfing makes me feel very small and very free. It reminds me of the profundity of nature and my connection with the whole. Both mushrooms and surfing make me bounce up.

The more you consider different ideas and participate in whatever actions that allow you to bounce up, your entire perspective will begin to take shape and mold into something less limiting. Soon, this higher-level thinking won't seem so difficult to achieve. It becomes ingrained in you. Earthly concerns might still bring you down, but you'll bounce back up more quickly. This shift in perspective allows a clearer mind and a greater sense of ease where life not only seems less overwhelming, but also just more enjoyable.

Chapter 10

The Meaning of Life

This is the age-old question, isn't it? Everyone thinks the answer is *so* elusive and deserving of hours of debate by our greatest scholars and philosophers, but in my opinion, the meaning of life lies with the ancient sages. Pick up any book on Eastern theology and you'll get your answer: Self-realization.

I understand that this whole concept of Self-realization is incredibly broad, and yes, thousands of books have been written on the subject and I suppose that some information in said books could potentially be up for debate. But let's make it easy on ourselves. This book is an overview, a mere survey of spirituality, a new lens in which to see the world. So, again, let's start with what we know.

In observance of the quintessence of the number one, we know that our soul, as an extension of Source energy, yearns to return back home. But in order to do that, the journey is long. We've lived thousands and thousands of lives in order to expand our inventory of knowledge. Source is the energy of total union and universal truth. We, as souls embodied, must undergo every realm of existence in order to actually understand every set of conditioning that is out there.

For example: In order to learn "loneliness," I might choose a life where, as a kid, I move around a lot. But that's not enough. So in another life, maybe I meet my soulmate when I am fifteen and he dies suddenly and I never love anyone else in that same capacity ever again. And in another life, I might be an orphan and so on and so on and so on. And even then, I still haven't fully integrated the concept of loneliness until I've lived hundreds of lives where I feel alone by every possible definition and iteration of the term.

Eventually somewhere within these lives, I finally begin to accept the idea that yes, I feel lonely, but perhaps, I can actively work to change that feeling. Born into lonely existences, I learn to surround myself with good people and suddenly I don't feel so alone. I've developed empathy for the experience of loneliness and I have also learned to combat it. This is how we realize our lessons.

It's the act of raising our individual and collective frequencies through empathy. We choose our lives so that we might fill in our gaps of knowledge and understanding.

When a person responds to the joys and sorrows of others as their own, he has attained the highest state of spiritual union.
The Bhagavad Gita

The Bhagavad Gita focuses on the development of empathy through selfless service in order to release karmic debt. Buddhism teaches the Eightfold Path as the key to end personal suffering and the cycle of reincarnation. Taoism asks that we, as individuals, work to become a receptacle for universal soul energy to perform its work through us.

At their core, all these faiths deliver the same message, but how can we bring this mission forward to the 21st century and utilize it in our everyday lives?

This might sound familiar: Self-realization on the singular life scale is a person consciously efforting towards their own betterment. It's our personal work. We use whatever proven tools and techniques to help us understand from where—and why—we come. We fight to understand our first nature—our reactions—and then we consciously advocate for a more beneficial second nature—who we want to be. By continually practicing reaction, awareness, and re-creation every time the opportunity arises, we become third nature beings—constantly aware and constantly improving. With these increments of improvement happening day in and day out, we start peeling back our own layers and we understand who we actually are beneath our external circumstances. We uncover our soul within as we learn our lessons and integrate this sense of universal empathy into our awareness.

This work will continue to change and pile on the more you engage in it. Because of this counterintuitive paradox, we must accept the idea that this path doesn't end anytime soon and instead practice gratitude for the work and the opportunity to grow. Some days it will be exhausting. When grace arrives, let it totally wash over you. Absorb yourself in it so that you can surface ready to take on the next cycle of effort. This is the path to Self-realization on the microcosmic, singular-life scale.

If you're ready to work on the macrocosmic scale of your eternal evolution then know that it's actually going to look relatively similar. You're on this field trip to learn these specific lessons that will help to fill in your entire web of knowledge. So it's okay and quite right to place attention in this life. You'll definitely catch larger-scale glimpses of your soul's path and mission whether it be through meditation, spiritual readings, or intuitive feelings. This information, however, mostly comes through to inform your present. Any work that you perform on the microcosm of this life is most certainly contributing to your overall macrocosmic path.

Self-work and learning our lessons is a personal inward path, but equally as important is figuring how to live out our quest for Self-realization in our external environment. It makes no sense to do all this personal excavating—uncovering your darkest demons and lighting them on fire—if you don't take what you've uncovered and utilize it in the world. This is why we're embodied. We're supposed to enact our gifts in the physical realm here on earth.

Selfless work is a concept mentioned frequently across all

faiths. From my Episcopalian childhood, the phrase, *"Go in peace to love and serve the Lord,"* comes to mind, mainly because that was the indicator that church was over and maybe we would get Krispy Kreme on the way home. We don't need to serve anyone, that's just religious vernacular. Instead, we allow Source energy to emanate through us by performing selfless work.

Remember, we are not individual beings. We never have been. We are Source particles caught beneath the Veil of Maya. We feel separate and distinct, but that's delusion talking. As tiny snippets of Source energy, what we truly want is to act out Source's will, whatever that may be, and return home in some glorious reunion. But it's super complicated down here. The density and negative energies of earth make us forget and drive us back towards ground-level thinking.

Under the lens of Taoism, which automatically means a more ambiguous description, we have the following:

Therefore all things arise from the Tao.
By Virtue they are nourished,
Developed, cared for,
Sheltered, comforted,
Grown, protected.
Creating without claiming,
Doing without taking credit,
Guiding without interfering.
This is the Primal Virtue.
Tao Te Ching, Ch. 51

This passage tells us that Source, or the Tao, is innately good. Humans, by their soul, arise from the Tao, so we, too, are innately good. Deeply rooted in human nature is the desire to do good for the greater good. I understand that might not always seem apparent from our ground-level thinking, but I trust the sages. By exercising these intrinsic motivations, a soul performs the Tao's work and is therefore protected. This work is just as imperative on our paths to Self-realization. Here it is said again in *The Gita*:

> *At the beginning, mankind and the obligation of selfless service were created together.*
> **The Bhagavad Gita**

We all want to return home, it is our most deeply rooted and primal instinct as souls embodied. Selfless service is a way towards that goal. In doing our personal work, we begin to understand our soul and its mission. From there, we might start to realize how we can best offer up our gifts and talents in order to effect positive change on a scale larger than ourselves.

I am a born seeker. I am deeply curious, and along with Self-realization, I hold universal exploration as my highest priority. My gifts include a certain amount of fearlessness that allows me to explore unknown territory and the ability to write about it in a way that delivers a concise and accessible message.

I admire vigilantes, the ones who never fail to speak up whenever they witness an injustice. For a long time, I wished that I, too, could be a vigilante, but I realized that it simply doesn't coincide with my gifts. My talents make me better for discovery, contemplation, and sharing what I've learned through writing. I can't confidently tell people off, and doing so wouldn't be reflective of my nature. I will, however, always admire my super dope friends who are qualified and have the ability to make others question their actions with intelligence and grace.

As you continue your self-discovery, start to ask yourself where you can best contribute your abilities to the greater whole. If you're applying for a job in marketing, maybe skip the interview for the giant corporation whose parent company is largely responsible for poisoning the oceans. Instead, apply for the nonprofit or the company that actively donates to the

World Wildlife Fund. On a smaller scale, do some research on the brands that you support or the products that you buy. Make sure their mission involves some degree of altruism over greed. It might take a little more effort and there might be some sacrifices that you decide to make, but that's the name of the game in selfless service. It's not supposed to be easy.

That being said, take care of yourself. We've chosen a difficult path, so self-care is crucial. Get really good at becoming aware of your extremes and know what it takes to strike a healthy balance. You're going to go through some really rough patches that will lead to episodes of profound growth. During these times, nurture yourself. Go easy on yourself. Remember that it's not selfish to take some time alone or some time off. This awareness will serve not only you, but those around you. You don't have to explain yourself or prove yourself. When you act from your center—all external forces removed—your soul takes the driver's seat and all that soul wants is whatever is best *for you*. Finally, acknowledge any gain, big or small, and always, almost obsessively, utilize the tools that bring you joy.

While we often think of Self-realization as a very personal journey, remember that in actuality, it's not a path we walk alone. My evolution directly depends on yours where we end this crazy goose chase in a complete and collective merge within the whole. All of us have a role to educate ourselves and uplift one another.

Live out your lessons and live up to your own sense of righteousness. It sounds like a lot, but it's not something that needs to be done all at once. Find the balance between the inward work and the outward work and let the lessons on each side commingle and inform the other. Start small with whatever tangible step feels right and the rest will absolutely unfold—in time. Patience is also key.

Metaphorical Analysis Alert!

Imagine a plateau where the flat top is the destination. It is the universal whole of consciousness; the most elusive realm; the One; the Source. We are the climbers—every single speck of consciousness here on earth, in a parallel universe, in another galaxy, in another realm, literally *every* single speck of energy that holds even an ounce of consciousness—we're climbing the plateau.

We all start off at different places on our individual climbs. Some on the northside, others on the southside. Some crawl out of a cave. Whatever. We ascend this plateau at different speeds. Some of us are just faster, others got a head start, some are just ancient old badasses and have been climbing for eons. And then there are the tiny, little, new baby souls too busy crying about their blankies to even begin their ascent. We're like little dots covering the entire surface area of this plateau representing every single circumstance of existence. There's a lot of variance, but we're all working together.

There is no one path up, but instead there are an infinite number of ways to get to the top and achieve Self-realization. Maybe you start on the northside, zigzag your way east, backtrack and then find a jetpack and zoom up a couple thousand feet, jetpack dies and you fall to the ground right back where you started before this whole insane detour ever occurred. As we climb, each individual soul brings their unique experience to the table, where no two souls have forged the same path. At the top, we dine together with every conceivable morsel of varying existence.

Some of us might have an affinity towards life on earth, while others prefer to reincarnate in other realms or galaxies. Whatever we choose and wherever we are, we're gathering the nuts and fruits of existence. Once we merge together, everything is at the table. So if you like a well-rounded potluck as much as I do, you can see why my evolution depends on yours. If you also hate the latecomers that make you sit and wait to eat, then you see why we all must arrive. This is why we should caravan, stick together, and help each other along the way. This is why we perform selfless service and practice empathy. We all bring our different dishes and gifts to the table so that once we all arrive, we may sit and dine together awashed in eternal peace.

Chapter 11

Tie a Bow Around It

One who sees himself as everything
is fit to be guardian of the world
One who loves himself as everyone
is fit to be teacher of the world.
Tao Te Ching, Ch. 13

This is it—the last chapter. Call it a review crash-course in spirituality. We've covered a lot of topics but really, we've only scratched the surface. There is an overwhelming amount of information out there, so luckily for us, our pursuits never have to end. We need only forge our paths. With all the spiritual texts that I've read, I always mark them up and dog-ear the pages that I want to return to whenever I am in a pinch and I need some quick hit of inspiration. It's nice to leave with some very clear and distinct takeaways to flip back to, so hopefully this chapter can serve that purpose.

First and foremost, I want you to remember that nothing I wrote here really matters. It's just an option. It's ultimately up to you whether or not you want to utilize the concepts, ideas, and tools outlined in this book. Maybe you made it to the end and you decide that it's just not your schtick. That's just fine. In the end, if you want to become a better person, you're going to do it in a way that is relevant to you on your path navigating this life.

The core of what we have learned and what these ancient texts and sages have taught us is that we're all part of the same organism, interrelated, connected and alike. The very essence of my soul has the same mission and the same desires as your soul. I don't only hope to attain my own Self-realization, but I need you to attain yours.

Every speck of consciousness is on the same team and I know that might be hard to believe considering the mass amounts of polarization in this world, but these great divides are inherent in nature—the number two. As long as we're existing here on earth, we're constantly combatting maya—delusion—and maya will always try to hold us back and make these divides seem impenetrable. If we approach division and resistance as tools for learning, then we're onto something. If we remember that a force called maya exists all around us, then we can better hold up our shields and defend ourselves.

Awareness is key. We need to stop living absentmindedly. Implicit energies are the driving force beneath all that happens to us. Some energies work for the negative, others for the positive. As humans with consciousness, we exert a profound amount of influence over the implicit forces that come into contact with us. With the right tools and practice we can protect ourselves from the negative and utilize all the forces that seek to help us. Awareness allows us to first notice what we are coming into *contact* with, and from there, we decide what to do with it. Thought drives energy. If we want less insecurity, we can meditate with, "I am secure in myself." If we want a teacher to come in so that we can learn a new technique, we will say, "I'm ready for my teacher." Manifestation is a real thing and all it takes is the right intention.

Remember also, that the helpful forces will send people and experiences your way in order for you to realize your lessons. Treat everyone with respect and gratitude because you don't know what lesson they may be delivering.

Move through your life with conscious awareness. Notice the patterns. Notice the energies that are particularly drawn to you. Notice the people coming in that uplift you. Notice those who create resistance in you. Just notice them and information will come flooding in as long as you remain receptive.

Self-realization is two-fold. Understand and know your innerworkings and then take your gifts and enact your soul's will upon the world. All our paths will look vastly different, but despite the variance, one thing is universal to all—we are One. The negative energies that occupy earth want us to fight each other, to resent each other and to separate ourselves. We can combat these forces by practicing empathy and understanding. The sages call it undivided love.

This supreme Lord who pervades all existence, the true Self of all creatures, may be realized through undivided love.
The Bhagavad Gita

One of the most profound messages I have ever received was towards the beginning of my conscious activity on this path. It was when I was living in Los Angeles and just exploring all my various options in the world of spirit. A friend and I had traveled deep into the valley all the way from the westside to a metaphysical shop. I had no idea what I was getting into and was excited but also slightly reluctant to walk into a room where the majority of the group considered themselves witches and warlocks—they were the real deal. We arrived, conversed, browsed books, and were finally brought up to the room where the Spirit Quest would take place. There was one man who stood in the corner the whole time who didn't participate because his specific role was to ward off any negative or harmful spirits that might try to creep in. Some of us stood, I sat down, we lit candles and in just a few minutes the leader was screaming and stomping around the room as if he were possessed. He was already in the other realm and leading the rest of us through this spiritual journey.

From what I recall, my body felt dense and heavy. I felt a heavy pressure slink over my shoulders and I intuited it to be the weight of the world. It exhausted me, all of humanity's suffering. I wanted to cry. At the close of the quest, our leader told us to receive the messages for which we came. I heard, "Divine Amnesty."

The faiths speak of love as the unifying force of consciousness, but to me we need to break it down a little bit. How can we love everyone and everything that crosses our path? How can I love a racist or a misogynist? How can I love an abusive husband or the ex-boyfriend that broke my heart? We don't need to hug and kiss them and pinch their little cheeks and tell them that we love them. All we have to do is understand their very unique point of view and what underlying factors have shaped them.

Someone quite close to me staunchly opposes everything that I believe in and hold to be moral and true. We literally do not align on any topic. I find him corrupt and ignorant and I am sure he finds me radical and arrogant. Part of me wants to abandon him, the other part of me wants to fight him. Instead, I have to constantly practice understanding. His upbringing shapes his views. His parents taught him his ethics. His culture defined the rules. And yes, of course you could make the argument that it is up to the individual to educate themselves and become well-rounded, but what if no one taught them how to even do that? What if their perception of well-rounded is different from yours? And when all else fails, bounce up to the soul-perspective. Some great and wise souls incarnate with the sole intention of driving chaos in order to create a mirror for you to learn your lessons. Motivated by true and evolved selflessness, this is an advanced soul.

So maybe this person—this agitator—came into my life to deliver a lesson, or perhaps even I came into their life to act as a mirror of reflection for them. We all encounter each other at different phases of our evolution. If you're a steadfast learner, then you keep up the hard work until you reach a place of understanding. If you're a teacher, then you don't turn your students away. Instead, you'd simply do your best to understand them and let the rest work itself out.

The inward path of Self-exploration means that the lessons and insights that you receive are yours and yours alone. What this also means is that you will never be capable of understanding exactly why another person is the way they are, therefore you can't judge it. Similarly and on the same note, you can't force people to learn their lessons. For a while in the beginning, I was so stoked on this new way of thinking—it had helped me so much and provided me with invaluable insights. Remember the boyfriend to whom I force-fed *Journey of Souls*? Take it from me, don't force it. It's their path to uncover. So you see, there are a lot of responsibilities in taking up this path and the most valuable tool for any of us is always going to be understanding.

At the time, I didn't know what amnesty meant, but after googling the definition, it all came into view. Amnesty is a pardon or forgiveness. Source energy, otherwise known as God or the Divine, grants each and every incarnating soul amnesty for their human actions. Whatever wrongs we end up doing throughout our lives, the bad decisions we make, the people we hurt, it's all forgiven in the eyes of the Divine. And it makes sense right? Under the Veil of Maya, we forget who we truly are. Earth is fucking hard. Our decisions and behaviors are all manifestations of our souls trying to discover themselves in a foreign body—to learn and explore. A lot of the time, mistakes lead to insight and are therefore necessary on our path of evolution. This is why we're forgiven. Like kindergartners on the playground, we're doing the best we can with what we know.

This is why we forgive each other and practice empathy. We are all a part of the divine. We're all headed to the same place. We all have our own lessons and obstacles that we need to work out in order to get there. The more we uncover our true Selves, the easier it will be to remember the innate instincts of our souls— to realize the Divine Amnesty within ourselves. This is what is meant by undivided love.

So here's the catch—full disclosure—by embarking on this path, there is no turning back. There have been so many times where my life has seemed unceasingly difficult, no grace in sight, the work was too hard and overwhelming and treacherous, and I would think to myself, "Why the fuck did I ever think that I wanted this?" The ignorance of not knowing truly is bliss.

Pre-path-of-Self-realization, I knew nothing about myself or my patterns. I approached the world with a laidback sense of nonchalance and carelessness. My motto for about two years was, "Whatever." Do you realize what that says about me at the time? I had a lot of skeletons in my closet and I was too afraid to confront them so instead I said, "Whatever," and pretended not to care. Life was hard back then, but easy in the sense that I didn't really understand what was so hard about it. I got pushed around by people, energies, situations, and my own ignorance towards my circumstances. Now, my mind follows a cycle of never-ending self-analysis in attempts to uncover more. I've ditched that old motto, and in turn, found my unshakable sense of motivation. I care about my priorities in a way that I never did before. The more I understand myself, the less I wish I could go back to before this all started. In a strange way, life is even more challenging now considering the effort that I put into it, but this time around, I'm in control. I want the hard work. I want to grow. I don't want to be compliant to my surroundings anymore. I'm currently at a point where I constantly acknowledge my gratitude for the work. Self-understanding is imperative. Meditation is dope. All my friends live in the astral. And life not only makes sense to me but it's also unbelievably exciting.

I'm not going to paint a pretty picture of love and peace. Yes it's out there, but as you've seen, it doesn't come easy. It gets really overwhelming but that's why we have our tools. It gets easier too in the joy that it brings. You can never turn back because you can't undo the progress that you've already made. You are a human being and with that comes free will. You can always choose to step off your path, but I guarantee you that your guides are going to bombard you with encrypted messages to get you back on track—that ignoring them would take even more work. In the end, your soul chose this life. It knows what it's doing. You're also profoundly taken care of and you're never alone. There is an entire network of energy constantly surrounding you and supporting you. Sometimes you can hear them cheering for you.

So the path is up to you, wherever you are. You don't have to live a spiritual existence if you don't want to. But you can try to live a more engaging life. Use the teachings in ways that make sense to you. Try to find balance between your extremes and cultivate new tools. Meditate. That's all it really takes to forge a path of self-work and become a better person. The world needs better people right now.

Mahatma Gandhi, we haven't heard from him yet, so real quick— another sage, promoted nonviolent resistance, rescued India from harsh British colonization, social and political activist, super cool dude. This is what he has to say about saving the world:

I have found that life persists in the midst of destruction. Therefore there must be a higher law than that of destruction. Only under that law would well-ordered society be intelligible and life worth living. If that is the law of life we must work it out in daily existence. Wherever there are wars, wherever we are confronted with an opponent, conquer by love. I have found that the certain law of love has answered in my own life as the law of destruction has never done... Every problem would lend itself to solution if we determined to make the law of truth and nonviolence the law of life.

Buddha taught that the root of all evil lies in greed, hatred, and delusion. These are the forces that lead man towards violence, corruption, and the infliction of undue suffering, which are unfortunately also the tenets of evil in our modern society. On an individual basis, be particularly weary of these forces: greed, hatred, and delusion. Humanity is not going to change when morality is not practiced and exhibited by world leaders and others in positions of power. A healthy sense of spirituality, morality and empathy will go a long way in affecting the future. We're the next generation once all these old, corrupt geezers die off. I truly believe that we can affect what comes next by learning the proper tenets of how to live now. We like Earth! Our souls certainly do, so let's not ruin it.

By establishing ourselves on the path of Self-realization, we create a blueprint for others to follow if they so choose. Do the work and figure out how to perform selfless service. Creation, preservation, destruction. Destruction leads to rebirth. We're in the midst of destruction, but I see creation on the horizon. We can be the creators of a new earth as long as we stay on the path and conquer it by undivided love.

To-Ponder List

When you approach something from a spiritual mindset, positive energies will make sure you get what you need out of it. If there was any lesson for you in between these two covers, I hope it stood out. So here it is, your final chance to ponder and reflect.

- **Define your belief system.** Did it shift at all? Do you need to do a little more inquiry? What really resonated? What do you want to explore further? What will you read next? What will you do next?
- **What are your primary lessons?** Where do you want to improve personally or spiritually?
- **What are your strengths?** Where can you best contribute to the world that is within your means and circumstance? What do you care about above all else?
- **What else can you add to your personal excavation?** What circumstances have shaped you? What patterns exist in your life that beg to be acknowledged and why? Who are you when every external idea, concept, or material thing is stripped away? In what areas can you do better? What can you contribute to the betterment of your community, your city, your country, or the world?

Endnotes

1. When I first got into yoga, I studied a theory called Katonah Yoga created by Nevine Michaan. Something very unique to her practice is that she infuses the theory with potent metaphors, some of which I refer to in this book. They shall henceforth be referred to as, "Nevine-isms."

2. This is not intended to offend any religious practitioner but rather refers to the history of corruption in various organized religions (i.e., Roman Catholic priests requiring payment to forgive sins in the form of indulgences and then personally pocketing that money).

3. *The Jap Ji*, a spiritual text based on the teachings of Guru Nanak, refers to this religious undoing in a really clear and concise overview in the book's introduction, written by Kirpal Singh.

4. Not to be confused with the denim company.

5. I'm too young for this, but you know what I am not too young for? *30 Rock*—where it was referenced one time.

6. For all of your Sacred Geometry needs, I recommend starting with *A Beginner's Guide to Constructing the Universe*, by Michael Schneider.

7. Ariyapariyesana Sutta (MN 26)

8. I once took a course on psychic healing with a teacher that I came across when I was living in Boise, ID. I learned about these energies from her teachings.

9. And for all your seasonal needs, my favorite book is *Staying Healthy with the Seasons*, by Elson Haas. This book is an integrative approach on medicine through the lens of both Eastern and Western healing traditions.

10. *The Emerald Tablet: Alchemy of Personal Transformation* by Dennis William Hauck

11. Billy Carson is another *Emerald Tablet* genius. He devotes

much of his time to researching and teaching the lessons and history of *The Emerald Tablet*.

12. I first read about this primary-school metaphor in *Journey of Souls* by Michael Newton. I have replicated it here and expanded upon it.

13. This is what Sri Yukteswar recounted to Paramahansa Yogananda which Yogananda later described in his book.

14. The realms are beyond my knowledge. As of right now, I believe that the three realms referred to here represent the lower three realms that are under the influence of the negative force, otherwise known as the Veil of Maya. There are then more realms above these three but they are of a much higher frequency and are rarely accessed by an embodied human soul.

15. 1st, 2nd, and 3rd natures are another Nevine-ism and this is my interpretation and application of their meaning.

16. Sidenote: Believe it or not, I was on the Varsity lacrosse team. Position played: videographer.

17. I'm calling it passive meditation for our purposes here but know that nothing about meditation is passive. It is very hard work.

18. Magga-Vibhanga Sutta (SN 45:8)

19. I first did this meditation with that same teacher from the psychic healing class.

20. Referenced in *Journey of Souls*.

21. Lessons from the psychic healing class.

22. Now streaming on Netflix.

23. Unknown origin.

24. There are so many books on Jung but a great intro would be *Jung's Map of the Soul: An Introduction* by Murray Stein. Although, if you really want to go deep, you could always go for *The Red Book* written by Jung himself.

25. Maslow first proposed his Hierarchy of Needs in a 1943 paper entitled, "A Theory of Human Motivation."

26. Nevine-ism

27. Important side note: If you want to differentiate Harry Potter magic from real-life magick, don't forget the "K."

28. The Veil of Maya is a concept mentioned all across spiritual texts. Of the resources mentioned in this book, you can learn more about maya in *The Bhagavad Gita*, *Autobiography of a Yogi*, *In the Buddha's Words*, and *The Jap Ji*.

29. Souls are androgynous, but in my mind, my soul is a tiny little boy.

30. Nevine-ism

References

Bodhi, B. (Ed.) (2005) *In the Buddha's Words: An Anthology of Discourses from the Pāli Canon*. Somerville, MA: Wisdom Publications.

Easwaran, E. (2007) *The Bhagavad Gita*. Berkeley, CA: Nilgiri Press.

Estés, CP (1995) *Women Who Run with the Wolves: Myths and Stories of the Wild Woman Archetype*. New York, NY: Ballantine Books.

Gaia Staff (2020, March 3) Gaia [Online]. Available at https://www.gaia.com/article/emerald-tablet-101-the-birth-of-alchemy (Accessed 17 July 2020).

Gandhi, MK (1972) *Gandhi: Truth is God*. Guelph, Canada: Alive Press.

Guru Nānak, & Singh, K. (1995) *The Jap Ji: The message of Guru Nanak; literal translation from the original Punjabi text with introd., commentary, notes, and a biographical study of Guru Nanak*. Irvine, CA: Ruhani Satsang Books.

Haas, EM (2003) *Staying Healthy with the Seasons*. New York, NY: Celestial Arts.

Hauck, DW (1999) *The Emerald Tablet: Alchemy for Personal Transformation*. New York, NY: Plume.

Jung, CG (2014) *The Collected Works of C.G. Jung Complete Digital Edition* (936667487 732749476 G. Adler, 936667488 732749476 M. Fordham, & 936667489 732749476 H. Read, Eds.; 936667490 732749476 RF Hull, Trans.). Princeton, NJ: Princeton University Press.

Lao Tsu (1989) *Tao Te Ching* (936595572 732706871 G. Feng, 936595573 732706871 J. English, & 936595574 732706871 T. Lippe, Trans.; 936595575 732706871 J. Needleman, Ed.). New York, NY: Vintage House, a division of Random House.

Newton, M. (1994) *Journey of Souls: Case Studies of Life Between*

Lives. St. Paul, MN: Llewellyn Publications.

Patañjali (2012) *The Yoga Sūtras of Patañjali* (936671145 732751509 S. Satchidananda, Trans.). Yogaville, VA: Integral Yoga Publications.

Schneider, MS (1995) *A Beginner's Guide to Constructing the Universe: The Mathematical Archetypes of Nature, Art, and Science*. New York, NY: Harper Perennial.

Yogananda, P. (1998) *Autobiography of a Yogi* (13th ed.). Los Angeles, CA: Self-Realization Fellowship.

Recommended Reading

Wisdom Texts:
The Bhagavad Gita – Eknath Easwaran
Tao Te Ching – Lao Tsu
In the Buddha's Words – Bhikkhu Bodhi
The Jap Ji – Kirpal Singh
Autobiography of a Yogi – Paramahansa Yogananda

Soul Exploration:
Journey of Souls – Michael Newton
Destiny of Souls – Michael Newton
Same Soul, Many Bodies – Brian Weiss
Messages from the Masters – Brian Weiss

Miscellaneous – Fun and Informative:
I Ching – Huang
Women Who Run with the Wolves – Clarissa Pinkola Estés
How to Change Your Mind – Michael Pollan
The Convoluted Universe – Dolores Cannon
A Beginner's Guide to Constructing the Universe – Michael Schneider
Staying Healthy with the Seasons – Elson Haas

BOOKS

O-BOOKS

SPIRITUALITY

O is a symbol of the world, of oneness and unity; this eye
represents knowledge and insight. We publish titles on general
spirituality and living a spiritual life. We aim to inform and help
you on your own journey in this life.
If you have enjoyed this book, why not tell other readers by
posting a review on your preferred book site?

Recent bestsellers from O-Books are:

Heart of Tantric Sex
Diana Richardson
Revealing Eastern secrets of deep love and intimacy to Western couples.
Paperback: 978-1-90381-637-0 ebook: 978-1-84694-637-0

Crystal Prescriptions
The A-Z guide to over 1,200 symptoms and their healing crystals
Judy Hall
The first in the popular series of eight books, this handy little guide is packed as tight as a pill-bottle with crystal remedies for ailments.
Paperback: 978-1-90504-740-6 ebook: 978-1-84694-629-5

Take Me To Truth
Undoing the Ego
Nouk Sanchez, Tomas Vieira
The best-selling step-by-step book on shedding the Ego, using the teachings of *A Course In Miracles*.
Paperback: 978-1-84694-050-7 ebook: 978-1-84694-654-7

The 7 Myths about Love...Actually!
The Journey from your HEAD to the HEART of your SOUL
Mike George
Smashes all the myths about LOVE.
Paperback: 978-1-84694-288-4 ebook: 978-1-84694-682-0

The Holy Spirit's Interpretation of the New Testament
A Course in Understanding and Acceptance
Regina Dawn Akers
Following on from the strength of *A Course In Miracles*, NTI
teaches us how to experience the love and oneness of God.
Paperback: 978-1-84694-085-9 ebook: 978-1-78099-083-5

The Message of A Course In Miracles
A translation of the Text in plain language
Elizabeth A. Cronkhite
A translation of *A Course in Miracles* into plain, everyday
language for anyone seeking inner peace. The companion
volume, *Practicing A Course In Miracles*, offers practical lessons
and mentoring.
Paperback: 978-1-84694-319-5 ebook: 978-1-84694-642-4

Rising in Love
My Wild and Crazy Ride to Here and Now, with Amma, the
Hugging Saint
Ram Das Batchelder
Rising in Love conveys an author's extraordinary journey of
spiritual awakening with the Guru, Amma.
Paperback: 978-1-78279-687-9 ebook: 978-1-78279-686-2

Your Simple Path
Find Happiness in every step
Ian Tucker
A guide to helping us reconnect with what is really important in
our lives.
Paperback: 978-1-78279-349-6 ebook: 978-1-78279-348-9

365 Days of Wisdom
Daily Messages To Inspire You Through The Year
Dadi Janki
Daily messages which cool the mind, warm the heart and guide
you along your journey.
Paperback: 978-1-84694-863-3 ebook: 978-1-84694-864-0

Body of Wisdom
Women's Spiritual Power and How it Serves
Hilary Hart
Bringing together the dreams and experiences of women across
the world with today's most visionary spiritual teachers.
Paperback: 978-1-78099-696-7 ebook: 978-1-78099-695-0

Dying to Be Free
From Enforced Secrecy to Near Death to True Transformation
Hannah Robinson
After an unexpected accident and near-death experience, Hannah
Robinson found herself radically transforming her life, while a
remarkable new insight altered her relationship with her father, a
practising Catholic priest.
Paperback: 978-1-78535-254-6 ebook: 978-1-78535-255-3

The Ecology of the Soul
A Manual of Peace, Power and Personal Growth for Real People
in the Real World
Aidan Walker
Balance your own inner Ecology of the Soul to regain your
natural state of peace, power and wellbeing.
Paperback: 978-1-78279-850-7 ebook: 978-1-78279-849-1

Your Personal Tuning Fork
The Endocrine System
Deborah Bates
Discover your body's health secret, the endocrine system, and
'twang' your way to sustainable health!
Paperback: 978-1-84694-503-8 ebook: 978-1-78099-697-4

Readers of ebooks can buy or view any of these bestsellers by
clicking on the live link in the title. Most titles are published
in paperback and as an ebook. Paperbacks are available in
traditional bookshops. Both print and ebook formats are
available online.

Find more titles and sign up to our readers' newsletter at
http://www.johnhuntpublishing.com/mind-body-spirit

Follow us on Facebook at https://www.facebook.com/OBooks/
and Twitter at https://twitter.com/obooks